GW00864908

KEEPING
THE BALLS
IN THE AIR

To John and Shirley, with best wishes

Alan Francis

KEEPING
THE BALLS
IN THE AIR

ALAN FRANCIS

ATHENA PRESS
LONDON

ISBN: 978 1 84748 376 8

First published 2008 by
ATHENA PRESS
Queen's House, 2 Holly Road
Twickenham TW1 4EG
United Kingdom

Printed for Athena Press

To the two Marys:
My wife, Mary Francis, and Bryn's wife, Mary Williams.
Both assisted and supported during eight years' intensive activity
by their husbands, particularly at weekends when karate meetings
and competitions caused many absences from home.
Without this loyal support, life would have been difficult.

Preface

When visiting a 2007 summer Martial Arts exhibition in Docklands as the guest of Terry Wingrove, it was commented that there was no written record of British Karate Control Commission activity between 1969 and 1977, a peak period of rapid expansion. It was said that various versions existed, but these were somewhat clouded with the personal interest of each storyteller.

I was asked, as Chairman of the Commission during those eight years, to write about the early formation and development of British karate, competitively and politically: this I have tried to do.

In this book I have also written personal and anecdotal experiences about my years at school during World War II, my early employment in a bank, national service and the police service, all of which combined to shape my judgement.

The police experiences are separated into chapters designated by the police stations at which I served. At one stage, my career in the police became closely intertwined with martial arts. Mostly minor and selected from hundreds of incidents, the stories included indicate the style of working life colleagues and I led, and the need for reasonable and fair balance when dealing with events and people. The accumulation of these experiences, culminating during my Chairmanship of the BKCC, will indicate that simultaneously I had several demanding roles, all of which I enjoyed as I tried, like a juggler, to 'keep the balls in the air'.

Some of the stories may surprise and amuse. I ask you to accept the whole as a sincere account of events.

I am most grateful to Bryn Williams for permission to use his *Know Karate-do* book account of the 2nd World Championships finals; to Brian Hammond, Steve Arneil and Peter Jordan, whom I consulted on some points of detail. Ivy Sharp, one-time Deputy Alderman and member of the City of London Court of Common

Council, has given valuable advice. I shall always be appreciative of those who actively contributed to the benefit of karate during my years in the chair. You were a great team.

Alan Francis
1 August 2008

Contents

Introduction – The Early Years

I joined the Metropolitan Police in April 1950, a few days before my twentieth birthday, and after training at Peel House was posted to Cannon Row police station, Westminster, known as Royal 'A' Division. My memories of the next five and a half years include the Christmas theft of the Coronation Stone from Westminster Abbey, the funeral of HM King George VI and the Coronation of HM Queen Elizabeth II. Apart from general policing, attending ceremonial events like the Changing of the Guard and Trooping the Colour, I worked additionally on relief at the Royal Palaces and in the Houses of Parliament, memorising over one hundred car registration numbers* of royalty, cabinet ministers and VIPs, developing a good knowledge of London and its bus and train routes. It was a very rewarding time, with immense job satisfaction, and marked a vast change and improvement on my first job when leaving school at nearly sixteen, working in the India Department of Grindlay's Bank at 54 Parliament Street, SW1, opposite the Cenotaph. I was originally destined to go to India with the bank, but later there was loss of life and serious trouble on that subcontinent with the creation of Pakistan and division of India, necessitating a machine-gun post at the Delhi branch and general upheaval in the northern branches. I decided to stay in London.

Germany

From age eighteen, I experienced open-air life during national service in the RAF Police, training at Pershore, Worcestershire, then moving on to Cosford in Shropshire, and finally to

---

* Irish Republican Army (IRA) activity subsequently made personalised car numbers a security risk, and their use by high-profile people ceased, so this knowledge was rendered useless, though I still remember many of the registration numbers to this day.

Gütersloh, Germany, with 110 Provost Flight in the centre of the town. Working in Germany in 1949 was a huge experience. The population understandably was still in shock four years after the war. I saw the railway sidings at Hamm with hundreds of bomb craters, and in Hanover they were still finding dead under the ruins; one could see across the town. It was similar to the fire devastation of the Barbican, City of London. The war had been a debilitating tragedy for Europe.

British military, known as British Army of Occupation of the Rhine (BAOR), 'policed' the British Sector of Germany; British service personnel in turn needed 'policing' by military police. There was an RAF station at Gütersloh, flying Vampire jets, and the Royal Air Force occupied a military barracks nearby. I spent several nights in the barracks and was very impressed with the bedding provided for German troops. The pillows were of eiderduck down, enabling a good, soft sleep in contrast to the straw-filled hard pillows of the RAF. Here the Germans had got it right – important to promote proper sleep.

The Provost Marshal of the RAF, Air Commodore de Putron, instigated an award, known as 'The de Putron Trophy', for which all Flights competed, wherever there was a provost unit UK and overseas. He then inspected the Flights, including Middle and Far East. You can imagine the competition, for it was a feather in the cap of an ambitious Flight Lieutenant if his unit won the competition.

So we had two kits, one for show and one to use. The hairbrush in the 'show kit', for example, was unused so that human hair would not be found thereon. Everything was immaculate, including the drill. One day we were 'on show' in the town centre, with the Air Commodore inspecting, when all concerned became aware of an approaching, unaccompanied, noisy milk cart, going much too fast, hauled by a head-down trundling bull, not caring about the niceties of road safety and heading for the parade. Our right marker broke ranks, and with much presence of mind grabbed the approaching bull by the horns, wrestling it down, preventing chaos and possibly some injuries. He was highly commended; 110 Flight won the trophy and our Flight Lieutenant, a former Hull City police officer, was very pleased.

Back to Banking

After demobilisation I returned to Grindlay's Bank, but soon applied to join the Metropolitan Police. I had seen a lot of the police at Westminster, as Cannon Row and New Scotland Yard were just round the corner from the bank in Parliament Street. We were good customers of John's Café in Derby Gate, where I listened to and enjoyed conversation with hardened plain-clothes police. There was another reason for wishing to leave the bank. When the banking hall shut at 3.30 p.m. daily, most of the staff, many back from war and used to cheap cigarettes, would light up, and the smoke turned the air blue. I went home 'kippered'; my clothes smelled of stale tobacco smoke and I felt unclean. Being an office junior, my weekly job was to go to Smith's Snuff Shop in St Martin's Lane (near the National Portrait Gallery) to collect the bulk office order. Believe it or not, cigarettes were still in short supply, so this weekly deal was eagerly awaited by some male staff.

Police Interview

In 1950 there were entrance and medical examinations for police applicants, and I attended Beak Street, off Regent Street, London, to be interviewed by a selection board of six formidable men, chaired by a retired army colonel. The man in police uniform on the right of the board, at the conclusion of the interview, said, 'Give my best wishes to your father.' I was stunned. 'What name shall I give, sir?' I responded.

'Tell him Superintendent Evans,' he replied.

I went home thinking I could do without this, and asked my father about Superintendent Evans. My father said, 'He was the man who rescued you when you were ten.' Ten years previously, at two o'clock in the morning on 29 September 1940, Inspector Evans had carried me out of our then home at 66 Beverley Gardens, Wembley, which had received a direct hit by a wartime high explosive bomb. Robin, my brother aged six years, was rescued by a fireman. My mother lost her life, and six had been killed next door. It was a job interview I shall not forget.

Some WW2 Memories

Robin and I were lucky that our parents declined the school offer to evacuate us to Canada for the duration of the war. After family discussion, it was decided that we should stay in Wembley. On Friday, 13 September 1940, those who had elected to go to Canada left Liverpool for Vancouver on board the liner *City of Benares*, flagship of the Ellerman Lines. When 600 miles into the Atlantic, the submarine U48 fired three torpedoes in heavy seas, the third striking the ship, which sank in thirty-one minutes. Seventy-seven children died and the news was released on 23 September 1940.[*] There was one Wembley survivor (from thirteen). In 2000 we attended the final (60th) memorial service at the Church of the Annunciation, Wembley, and still keep in touch with Preston Park Primary School, where we were pupils. The school commemorates the event annually on Armistice Day.

There are clear memories of the wartime activity and disruption of our schooling. The Battle of Britain was being fought by day and there was regular bombing by night. After our home was demolished we temporarily moved to Croxley Green, Hertfordshire, from where I daily commuted back to school at Wembley. During air raids, the trains would travel very slowly. In October 1940, the London Docks and City of London were set on fire and the sky glowed red: this sight was visible far beyond Watford, for we stood in the back garden at Croxley Green to stare in awe and amazement, pondering what was happening to London.

I was nearly thirteen when I started a paper round from Rogers' Newsagents in Preston Road, Wembley. This gave me the early morning opportunity to collect shrapnel and later V-1 fragments. I accumulated an excellent collection, including parachute silk and cord from a mine. The V-1 pilotless planes were relentless. Though D-Day had taken place in June 1944, our troops did not overrun the V-2 rocket launching sites until March 1945. The final rocket of the war hit Orpington on 27 March 1945. Over 9,200 flying bombs – each containing 1,000 kg of high explosive – had been launched. Of these, 2,419 reached London, each being capable of inflicting heavy damage.[†]

---

[*] Source: Barker, Ralph, *Children of the Benares*, Avid Publications

[†] Source: Ogley, Bob, *Doodlebugs and Rockets*, Froglet Publications

We were in the choir at the Church of the Ascension, Wembley. The sermon of the Revd John Ginever was in progress on an autumn Sunday morning in 1944, when the unmistakable noise of a V-1 grew louder and louder, then started to splutter like a failing motorcycle engine. The pulse-jet engine stopped; then utter silence was followed by a huge explosion. Our church was undamaged, but I shall not forget how the congregation swayed, as if on a ship. We later heard that the Guards Chapel at Wellington Barracks, in another incident, had been hit by a V-1, killing fifty-eight civilians and sixty-three service personnel. On the paper round, I saw many V-1 'flying bombs'; one was so low that I could see writing in white chalk on the fuselage; it came down towards Harrow on the Hill.

A V-2 rocket weighed 13.6 tons, 9 tons of which was fuel and 1 ton explosive. It took four minutes to arrive from the launching site, travelling up to sixty miles high and at 3,600 miles per hour. There was no defence and no warning. 517 reached London out of 1,115 reported. I heard double explosions high in the sky when V-2 rockets were about. It was not until 1955 that I learned that these were 'sonic booms', as demonstrated at Farnborough Air Show, when planes flew through the sound barrier and a de Havilland 110, piloted by John Derry, disintegrated. Supersonic flights over land were thereafter banned.

In the police service I met many colleagues who had exceptional war records. As I got to know them, and as opportunity arose – usually on night duty – I used to steer the conversation to their war experiences. Some had been decorated for bravery. 'Jock' Heggie, a constable, working at the Houses of Parliament, held the Distinguished Flying Cross for his exploits in RAF Mosquito bombers. Statistically he should not have been alive. Bob Frith held the Distinguished Service Medal for his role in the Royal Navy when sinking a U-boat. Another colleague had been mentioned in despatches for commando work in Italy. I was a listener, not a talker, and very respectful of their exploits. I kept quiet about my experiences when delivering newspapers (!) but may have mentioned the awesome sight of a thousand American bombers, consisting of B-17 Boeing Flying Fortress, Lockheed Hudson, and B-24 Consolidated Liberator, all lit from underneath by the early morning rising sun. These planes, noisy and heavily laden with bombs, had assembled in the north and east of England and were heading south in support of the D-Day landings. Within one hour they would have been heavily engaged.

I have taken my family to the American Military Cemetery at Madingley, Cambridge (junction 13, M11), where 3,812 brave men have graves.

There is one wartime school experience I would like to relate, which indicates how in the last sixty years society has changed, especially in relation to health and safety. East Lane School, North Wembley, had a large sports field which received an abnormal number of incendiary bombs, jettisoned when a German aeroplane had been caught in searchlights. As pupils we lined up across the sports field with instructions to raise an arm if we saw an incendiary bomb hole. A clean hole of two inches diameter meant that the bomb was unexploded: a charred hole indicated the bomb had burnt out. When a pupil raised an arm the teachers blew whistles and our line of about 200 stopped. The hole was then logged; then a further whistle signalled slow progress could be made. I was not told the number of bombs logged but I believe it to be in the region of one hundred.

From Rowing to Judo

I was very happy and felt privileged to be in the London Metropolitan Police. On my first day of duty at Cannon Row, and under instruction, I had to relieve the traffic point officer at the junction of Derby Gate and Parliament Street, a few yards from Grindlay's. The office girls came out to watch from the bank balcony, adding to my embarrassment. I found that traffic did stop when I raised my arm... and I was warned by the senior constables to never turn my back on the traffic when on the point opposite Horse Guards Avenue/Whitehall, where motorists, looking at the horse guards on duty, might run me down! (Traffic lights have long since taken over; they do not get cold, tired or require a refreshment break.)

I had the novel experience of taking police examination papers to study, when convenient, inside 10 Downing Street, St James's Palace, the police box at Trafalgar Square, No. 1 Carlton Gardens, (home of the Foreign Secretary) and other establishments ideal for learning. One could be both alert and paid for studying at the same time!

George Chew, then 3rd dan and a British international judoka, was a senior constable at Buckingham Palace. Judo dan grades (black belts) were very rare in those days, and George Chew was viewed in some awe. One of his pupils, Constable Colin Cross, also of 'A' Division, and a 2nd kyu (blue belt), was also regarded in judo terms as 'senior'. Conversing with Colin on night duty finally caused me to join the London Judo Society (LJS). Hitherto I had been rowing at Putney and Hammersmith, first with the National Provincial Bank Rowing Club (Grindlay's was affiliated) and later with the Metropolitan Police Rowing Club. Though I had some memorable times at regattas, the difficulty with the police club was that shift work and unpredictable court appearances made assembly of a regular crew difficult. Several times, even off night work and before going to bed the same day, I had journeyed to the Thames at Hammersmith to find that seven men, the cox and the coach had arrived – but not the vital eighth man, who had been delayed dealing with a traffic accident or an unwelcome but necessary arrest! A racing 'eight' needs eight rowers, not seven or six, so Colin Cross, talking in the early hours, had little trouble in persuading me that judo was the answer: one could train alone or with two or more, making an absent member irrelevant.

There was another, more personal, reason. I was conscious that, though six feet tall, I might not, as a constable, be able to acquit myself well if called to a fight. I needed training, and judo amply provided this. I later ceased to worry, mainly because I was better able to keep the issue in correct perspective and would know what *not* to do, which was as important as knowing one's limitations and what to do.

On the Move and Back

The Prime Ministers during my service at 'A' Division were Clement Attlee, Winston Churchill and Anthony Eden. I saw them all when on duty inside and outside No. 10. By the time Harold Macmillan arrived I had already left the service.

I became restless. Pay for a constable was poor – in 1955 it was £450 a year. I felt the need to break out from the present role and try to earn more in the big wide world. I responded to an advertisement in the *Daily Telegraph*, went for three subsequent interviews (also just off Regent Street) and found myself at Bristol on New Year's Day, 1956, starting a new job as trainee representative. It paid well and included all hotel and travel expenses. I was excited. For a single man this was luxury, my total salary becoming pocket money. I enjoyed the huge learning curve, travelling the valleys of Wales, the Highlands of Scotland, the industrial Midlands, the North East and North West, and most of Great Britain's seaside resorts. I saw the whole country at work and banked sufficient money to put a substantial deposit on a house. This greatly affected my life and I worked for J S Fry and Sons of Bristol (Cadbury/Fry), a wonderful company and employer, for three and a half years.

However, I missed the police, the esprit de corps and general camaraderie. So, in July 1959, I was back in public service, my first love, but this time in the City of London Police, where my father and grandfather had served and my brother was serving. I missed the company car and all the expenses, and took a big salary drop, but resolved to renew studies and start afresh. Once again, I was very happy to be back in uniform renewing contact with the public. Now married, and with my wife expecting a child, I had additional responsibilities.

I much enjoyed judo and, following the three-and-a-half-year break with Fry's, I resumed training in 1959, forming the City of London Police Judo Club. Terry Wingrove, from a Snow Hill business next door, whom I was to meet in later years on World Karate matters, used to visit and train in Snow Hill police station, as did trainee doctors from St Bartholomew's Hospital. Digressing, when on night duty in Westminster in 1955 and patrolling Cockspur Street, SW1, I saw the following unusual notice on a blackboard in the window of the offices of the P&O Shipping Company: 'Special offer, first come first served. A few half-price vacancies on the SS *Arcadia*. Visiting Lisbon, Malaga, Madeira and Tenerife'.

The date coincided with my leave the following week. Off duty by six and in bed by half past, I got up at 9 a.m. (I lived at police accommodation in Ambrosden Avenue, Victoria) and by 9.30 had booked the cruise. I mention this because on the ship I found two other judoka, one a member of the crew. We set up mats on deck, and by loudspeaker challenged anyone on board to a contest. A few tried but even with little knowledge and skill we easily coped. To repeat that, fifty years on, would be crazy and invite disaster for the challenger! In 1963 by chance I again met the judoka passenger from the 1955 *Arcadia* cruise, who was now a Metropolitan Police officer. We arranged a team match in Snow Hill police station, including demonstrations of aikido, also kendo by Roald Knutsen of the British Kendo Association. The Commissioner, Sir Arthur Young, attended and the whole evening was successful, having evolved out of a coincidence.

The Metropolitan Police Judo Club had given me many ex-periences. I became George Chew's demonstration partner, taking hundreds of falls at fêtes, public exhibitions and judo shows, all excellent experience. I attended George Chew gradings at many judo clubs ranging from the Royal Military Academy, Sandhurst, to Cardiff Judo Club. The highest judo grade in South Wales in 1955 was 1st kyu (brown belt). I think George Chew, who knew my style and capabilities, deliberately kept me undergraded, so that he could judge and grade at various clubs using me as a 'standard'. I did not mind this at all; indeed it suited me, as I could 'freewheel' slightly with more senior grades, minus the stress and tension one would normally experience in *randori* (free practice). If you think this reads that I was easy-going on the tatami (mats) then you would be right – some would prefer to engage in a more fighting spirit.

I was sometimes at LJS early in the day before starting work. Members of Cyril Stapleton's BBC Showband, Sydney Lipton's Orchestra, Johnny Dankworth's Seven and others, Harry Leader and ace trumpeter Freddie Clayton, were pleased for the opportunity to train in the mornings, for they had long evenings ahead. We were given tickets to attend BBC broadcasts, and on Sunday evenings at the Camden Theatre we saw recordings of the legendary *Goon Show*. Peter Sellers was an LJS member, and, for connoisseurs of big band music, Tim Bell (double bass), Sid Holmes (trumpet), Laddie Busby and Bobby Micklebrough (trombone), all regular broadcasters, attended London Judo Society.

When at Cloak Lane police station in the City, I arranged my duties so that I could teach judo to the Whitbread Brewery apprentices at a regular weekly session. Afterwards we visited the 'City Cellars' below the brewery, where refreshment was available with no till in sight. Whitbread's were very helpful to karate in later years (described in the chapter on the 3rd World Championships).

By mid-1969 I was Chief Superintendent responsible for administration and training in the City of London Police, and at Christmas 1969 was posted to Wood Street police station, where I spent the next eight happy, hectic years. In the summer of 1969 George Chew telephoned. I owed him a lot, for he had unselfishly looked after me at LJS. I had given his bank a guarantee for the purchase and refitting of the London Judo Society at new premises at Stockwell, and had no qualms about this, for George Chew was steady as a rock and my house would not be at risk. He asked me to meet him and Len Palmer, Honorary Secretary of the British Karate Association, to discuss a proposition he would rather not declare on the telephone. I was curious but willing, having no idea what proposition awaited, and will write about the result in a later chapter, concerning the origins and development of the British Karate Control Commission... It affected my life considerably.

The London Judo Society and Kenshiro Abbe

The 1947 founders of the London Judo Society (LJS), originally called the 'South London Judo Society', were George Chew and Eric Dominy, both ex-Budokwai Judo Club and British team internationals. George Chew was an RAF parachute training instructor during the 1939–45 war, and Eric Dominy was in the army. Captured in the Italian campaign, Eric learnt his judo from fellow prisoner Percy Sekine (also Budokwai Judo Club) before successfully escaping in Italy and subsequently winning the Military Medal. He had represented Great Britain at athletics. They started the club with their demobilisation gratuities, borrowing several thousand pounds from four local friends – this debt being a large sum of money in the early 1950s, four years' wages for many.

If it comes to notice that one has banking/bookkeeping experience, there is high risk of being asked to become treasurer. In 1951 I became honorary treasurer of LJS and set about trying to repay these founding debts, at the same time developing policies to enlarge the club, moving all the activities into profit.

We advertised on London Underground trains, plus the two main London evening papers and, in conjunction with London County Council, ran evening classes and beginners' courses. It was highly successful and there were longish waiting lists for these eight- and twelve-week sessions.

Ichiro Hatta, 7th dan judo, Japan, used to visit London to buy Western-type films, staying with George and Joan Chew. When Ichiro Hatta visited LJS there was always immense interest and benefit and it was realised by all that if LJS could employ a resident senior Japanese instructor the club would prosper. As a result of the judo courses, we now had funds available to make this possible. In one year we were able to repay the debts, extend and refurbish the club, and launch enquiries for a senior instructor. George contacted an ex-British team colleague, now in

Argentina, and Kenshiro Abbe was recommended. He came with formidable credentials; I recall he was then Japan's senior 7th dan, judo; 6th dan, aikido; 3rd dan, kendo, and dan graded at Japanese chess, which I had not heard of before. He was once the youngest-ever Japan universities champion at 5th dan, judo, and had advised Japanese television on budo matters. Once a major in the Japanese army, and with subsequent police superintendent experience, he made a first-class candidate.

In 1954 I drove George Chew and Eric Dominy to Heathrow to meet Kenshiro Abbe from the overnight plane. I remember passing my driving test two days previously and hiring a Morris Oxford car for the Heathrow occasion. (I have since tried to establish the precise date of his arrival by asking the DVLA at Swansea for the date I passed the driving test. Alas, their records do not go back that far.) After greetings, a meal and a rest, Kenshiro Abbe made his first appearance at LJS, taking on every member of the club in one big line-up, one after the other. He demolished everyone very quickly, and his sweeping ankle techniques were so fast that we had difficulty in seeing and following the action. Kenshiro Abbe really was exceptional: this was judo as we had never seen before. He was taken to arranged accommodation in south-east London, his salary was assured, and he was also able to earn private fees from lessons at LJS and elsewhere.

I later had pleasure in writing his judo thoughts, at his request, on 'circular movement'. This was very enlightening. I remember him well: well dressed, polite and appreciative. My family was impressed when he visited my home, then in Bromley, Kent.

The British Judo Association was still in its infancy. Word was that they needed a treasurer, and that I would be proposed at the next Annual General Meeting at Kingsway Hall, London. I could not get off duty to attend the AGM on this Saturday afternoon, and to my surprise I was duly elected Honorary Treasurer of the British Judo Association whilst working a traffic point outside the Houses of Parliament! (No traffic lights then.) I produced the first fully audited accounts in the following year, but did not stand for re-election as I was considering leaving London to seek other employment. Nevertheless, I had an excellent year's experience in seeing the early workings of the BJA under the chairmanship of Wing Commander Barnes of the Budokwai; we got on well. Charles Palmer, later to become a distinguished BJA chairman, and Chairman of the British Olympic Committee, was in Japan.

The impact of Kenshiro Abbe was immense, and a whole range of new moves and techniques was taught. It was considered that his gradings were more generous than those awarded by George Chew and Eric Dominy, but all concerned were very pleased. He showed great courage in challenging the self-styled World Champion, 'Tiger' Joe Robinson, said to be 6th dan, to a contest at LJS. I was one of many who sat in awe of what was about to happen – my heart thumped so hard within my rib cage that I was conscious of it. Joe Robinson, immensely strong, and towering over Kenshiro Abbe, held him stiffly at arm's length, making it very difficult for Kenshiro Abbe to attack effectively, but he gamely had a good go with several techniques. At one time, Joe Robinson lifted Kenshiro Abbe off the ground. Eric Dominy refereed this match, which was declared a draw. Under current rules, Kenshiro Abbe may have been awarded the contest for attacking spirit, but that was not heard of then. Kenshiro Abbe was disappointed, but we thought he had shown true fighting spirit against unknown and powerful odds.

Kenshiro Abbe knew a mass of very simple, effective techniques. For example, I was originally taught that to evade the attack of *tsuri komi ashi* (drawing ankle throw) one should lift the leg to step over the incoming attack: this meant lifting the whole leg – tibia, fibula and femur; a lot of limb. Kenshiro Abbe taught that one should swing back the tibia and fibula only; in other words just swing back the lower leg, not moving the upper leg. It was much quicker, easier and more effective. Apart from judo, I have since applied this knowledge hundreds of times when stepping over low walls or fences. Why lift the whole leg?

Back at LJS, matters took an unexpected turn. Kenshiro Abbe, who had started to live mainly in his tracksuit, left his lodgings in south-east London and promptly moved his accommodation into the small 'canteen' at LJS in St Oswald's Place, Kennington, SE11, from where he held court and camped on a bedroll. George and Eric were not pleased, but one does not quickly act to evict the now 'fully resident' respected 7th dan whose skills were sought after… Quite a problem. It was a dilemma which got worse when Kenshiro Abbe brought tropical birds to the club: they multiplied and flew about the dojo. Birds make a mess and it became unpleasant. Ultimately he left the club in 1956. A discreet comment in the LJS publication, *Judoka*, simply reported that the club canteen 'had now returned to normal'. We all knew what it meant, a sad loss for everyone.

I have since read in Dr Clive Layton's book *Shotokan Dawn*, Volume 1, page 47, that Kenshiro Abbe returned to Japan after 1957, lonely and penniless, feeling exploited. I am so sorry to read of this. It occurs to me that a man of such superb and valuable talent needed a good manager and adviser – a great pity this did not happen. Having gone to work in Bristol in January 1956 I was out of touch with what then happened in London, so fifty years later this was a surprise revelation.

Kenshiro Abbe had also formed a British Judo Council, and a number of clubs joined, in spite of the fact there was already an officially recognised governing body for judo – the British Judo Association – of which the London Judo Society was a founder member.

BKCC Origins and Development

In the late 1960s a murder trial took place at the Central Criminal Court, Old Bailey, in which the accused's defence was that he had been taught karate and had no idea how effective his technique could be in application, as the decisive 'karate' blow on the deceased had caused an unintended result. The trial judge recommended an official inquiry into karate activity. The Department of Education and Science, the Central Council for Physical Recreation (later the Sports Council) and the Home Office all had an interest. New Scotland Yard was asked to conduct the inquiry. The report, simplified, recommended that karate activity was an acceptable and growing activity but that growth and development needed to be controlled.

All the main known associations were called to a meeting chaired by Sir John Lang at the Central Council for Physical Recreation (CCPR) and the British Karate Council Commission (BKCC) was formed with this official encouragement. It started slowly and there were arguments. Bruce Donn, a lawyer, was the first chairman, but he left to take up an appointment abroad; meanwhile Bryn Williams, liaison officer at the CCPR, recorded the meetings and became an unofficial interim chairman.

A proliferation of karate organisations had adopted 'British' titles, some giving the impression to the public that they had national status. The main known groups were:

British Karate Association	(BKA)	All styles
British Karate Federation	(BKF)	All styles but originally Shotokan
United Kingdom Karate Federation	(UKKF)	Wado-Ryu
Karate Union of Great Britain	(KUGB)	Shotokan

British Karate Kyokushinkai	(BKK)	Kyokushinkai
Shukokai Karate Union	(SKU)	Shukokai
Scottish Karate Association	(SKA)	All styles

and later:

British Karate-do Goju Ru kai	(BGA)	Goju-Ryu
Karate Union of Scotland	(KUS)	Shotokan

As implied in the previous chapter, I duly met George Chew and Len Palmer at the new London Judo Society premises at Stockwell. They explained their ongoing concern about the direction, or lack of direction, of the British Karate Control Commission, and said there was too much internal rivalry and animosity. At the CCPR on one occasion it was said the noise from within the committee room so concerned the lady with the tea trolley that she was frightened to knock and enter whereas, in fact, she would have been welcomed! George Chew and Len Palmer had, meanwhile, been to see Fred Peart MP* at the House of Commons. His advice was that in the first place a chairman, independent of karate, should be sought.

George and Len were now looking in my direction, a judoka, to be nominated as an independent chairman. George had an interest in that karate was now also being taught in LJS and he wished to put the karate club interests on a proper 'official' footing. Len Palmer's concern was the ongoing political and financial domination by Japanese instructors. I was assured that the role of chairman would necessitate 'a Sunday once every couple of months', so I agreed to be nominated.

I met Bryn Williams, now a Sports Council officer. In 1970 the Sports Council was established by Royal Charter, the CCPR staff joining the Sports Council en masse. The CCPR then became a separate forum for all governing bodies of sport, in the following divisions:

---

* Fred Peart was a highly regarded member of parliament: he became Leader of the House of Commons and subsequently Leader of the House of Lords.

- Games and Sports (the British Judo Association and the BKCC were in this Division)
- Outdoor Pursuits
- Movement and Dance
- Water Recreation
- Interested Organisations (I here represented the Police Athletic Association)

Bryn Williams was a London School of Economics graduate who had additionally graduated from Loughborough College, qualifying as a coach and referee in football and athletics activities. He had also started to practise Kyokushinkai Karate under Bob Bolton at the London Judo Society in the mid-1960s before moving to Hong Kong for two years where he studied a Chinese form of Wu Shu under Mr Wong Lun. This knowledge of style variety was to prove useful in a multi-style organisation like the BKCC.

Sir Walter Winterbottom, Sports Council Director, agreed to loan a 'portion' of Bryn to the BKCC to get it operational and Bryn duly coped with BKCC and other Sports Council work.

My first BKCC Sunday meeting took place at Wood Street police station in the City of London. Mr Clinton Sayer of the Sports Council opened the proceedings and I was then introduced and elected, finally getting down to business with first the accuracy of the minutes of the previous meetings. It was not easy. There were points of order, challenges, various motions and amendments, all of which had to be dealt with carefully to stand the test of time. Luckily I belonged to a group at the City Literary Institute called the Simpletons (based on **S**peech **I**n **M**anagement) which specialised in role play, the conduct of committees and procedures. Harry Cardwell was a leader of this group, and the father of John Cardwell – a prominent City of London Police swimmer. Little did I think I would 'go through the card' on procedure one Sunday afternoon! I returned home very tired, pleased I had met the members and realising there was an immense amount of work to do. This was not indeed a 'meeting every two months' job. I could see it was going to take a lot of thought and time. I had been handed a 'sword in a scabbard': the more I gently extracted the sword, the more formidable it appeared, quite a challenge. What I did, or did not do, with 'the sword' was going to be critical.

Bryn's work for BKCC was absolutely strategic, his forte being the ability to reduce the record of earlier bad-tempered and complicated meetings to a set of sensible minutes to be scrutinised, actioned and voted on at the next meeting. I cannot emphasise how helpful Bryn's ongoing ability, knowledge and advice came to be: we worked separately yet together, like two bowlers on a cricket field, one at the pavilion end and one at the gasworks end, both trying to achieve a result in the interests of the whole and sometimes switching ends. We were actually playing for the committee members though they did not at first appreciate this. In reality I worked from the 'City end' while Bryn worked from the 'Sports Council end'. Our whole objective was to establish credibility for karate, to help develop the activity in a controlled way, support and encourage all member organisations to follow a code of conduct and to foster a strong national competition team. We had fastened our seat belts and started.

The Scots complained bitterly that for each meeting they attended in London, air fares were a burden. At the first meeting a Scots voice called out, 'Mr Chairman, I want to know what right he (indicating a member) has to sit at this table?'

'What are we going to do about the cowboys already in our local sports centres when we are not allowed in?' demanded another.

Oh dear, there was a lot to do. If a motion had a seconder and if there were no other motions or amendments, we voted on it. A majority vote would carry the motion and we steadily got through the agenda. There were meetings with late finishes and my wife became used to it, and Sundays were so valuable. I was apologetic for the absences and she was very supportive.

Bryn lived in Eltham, south-east London, and I lived in Orpington, Kent. We more or less took it in turns to drive each other home from London and beyond, using this prime time to talk over the meetings and discuss the actions required. I could see that I was going to have to travel the country, to meet the members on their home ground, to see for myself, and try to achieve trust and a consensus. We just had to make progress fast.

I also met Brian Hammond, who was the BKCC Honorary Treasurer, a black belt in judo and karate, a travel agent (which was later strategically helpful) with a clever sense of humour. Brian also became a talented respected referee, well regarded in Europe. He was to play an important role.

Making the Time

In the police service the rank of superintendent and above carries a twenty-four-hour responsibility. In the city, chief superintendents were additionally on emergency call for one seven-day week in three, known as the 'Duty Division' and this was compensated by six weeks' annual holiday. I resolved to spend three weeks of this holiday with the family, and three weeks, taken in single or double days as required, on karate matters, visiting karate clubs and attending meetings around the country. A helpful letter, addressed to Commissioner James Page, from Sir Walter Winterbottom, asked that I be given support for this role as the Sports Council attached importance to the effectiveness of BKCC, which had hitherto been slow.

So it came to be that I embarked on a policy of personally visiting the members in their home areas. In management-jargon terms it was a classic situation requiring 'management by walking about'. I travelled a lot at weekends, receiving much courtesy, and was at once very surprised at the huge national growth in martial arts. Enthusiasm was bubbling everywhere. One hears of the lifelong loyalty of football fans to their chosen club: in some cases a fanatical loyalty fostered on the terraces, but the fierce loyalty of karate members to their style and to their instructors just had to be seen and experienced. It was reflected in their strong views at committee. I began to understand their points of view.

I also met three senior Japanese instructors in the City Friends restaurant, Old Bailey: Keinosuke Enoeda (KUGB), Tatsuo Suzuki (UKKF) and Mitsuske Harada (KDS) were all very cooperative. At the outset it was important to achieve a good understanding.

As each weekend meeting progressed, and we moved venues

round the country, the members got used to my style and the feeling was mutual. Meetings became more amicable. We paid for the Scots delegates' London fares as it would have been ludicrously expensive to take the whole Commission to Scotland. Therefore, Birmingham, Coventry, London, Nottingham and Manchester became favoured locations and in some cases, through liaison through police athletics secretaries, these meetings were held in police premises. London meetings were at Wood Street police station.

Underneath the surface there was still some rivalry and animosity. For example, at one UKKF event at Crystal Palace National Sports Centre, which was well organised and running smoothly, there were three telephone calls stating a bomb was due to explode. After the third evacuation I advised the management to ignore all further calls but maintain good security on the doors. A rival breakaway group was suspected. Incidents such as this lessened as time progressed but some damage was done to karate's overall credibility.

A cornerstone of BKCC policy was that style preferences were recognised and the specialist style groups were supported, but only one group per style. The exception was the 'all styles' British Karate Association and the British Karate Federation which was Shotokan originated but had long since lost the lead for that style.

I continued to visit karate clubs at their own dojos. On one occasion I telephoned Vernon Bell, founder of the BKF, to ask if I could attend his federation's advertised event with a group of city police cadets. He agreed. About twenty cadets came with two instructors – I considered it good experience for the cadets to watch an activity which would be completely new to them. Meanwhile, I sought out Vernon Bell. I found him agitated and worried. 'We're going to have trouble. The skinheads have arrived,' he said. I assured him that the 'skinheads' were police cadets and, Wellington barracks excepted, the best disciplined group in London. He then laughed and relaxed. The event was well presented and the cadets learned a lot just by watching.

I attended most of the associations' championships and a lot of their meetings. The most efficient and progressive organisation was the KUGB, specialising in Shotokan karate and with links to the Japan Karate Association. Their events attracted capacity crowds of supporters and their presentation matched the high quality of the karate – they had some style. They also helped with the organisation of BKCC championships, supplying referees, judges and officials for timekeeping et cetera. Their leader, Keinosuke Enoeda, was a superb athlete and demonstrator who tragically died prematurely from cancer; a great loss. Keinosuke Enoeda and his wife had been to some City Police social events and were much respected. The shotokan-style European Championships, held at Crystal Palace, were first class in organisation and presentation. Eric and Julia Morely, of Mecca and Miss World fame, together with Sir Arthur Young, ex-commissioner of police, attended and presented prizes. I also visited Marshall Street Baths in Soho with Sir Arthur Young to watch Keinosuke Enoeda take a KUGB class workout. We were very impressed.

At the same technical level was the UKKF, specialising in Wado Ryu karate. Professor Tatsuo Suzuki was their chief instructor. He had been a professor of physical training in Japan and gave precise, slick demonstrations with his colleague Japanese instructors at the UKKF events. The secretariat of UKKF and officials also gave generously of their time at BKCC events.

The Karate-do Shotokai members were fortunate to have Mitsusuke Harada of Japan (now a British subject) as their founder and chief instructor. Shotokai I saw as 'karate for the thinking man' specialising in kata, non-competitive, and having main bases in universities where Harada built up a loyal, dedicated and very respectful following. I visited well-attended KDS events in Newcastle, Warwick and Canterbury which were very well run. KDS were always polite in committee and willing to contribute. I still keep in touch with KDS and Mitsusuke Harada, now resident in Wales, who has a loyal following in Europe. In 2007 he was awarded a well-deserved MBE for his services to karate.

Steve Arneil led the BKK which was respected as a hard, tough style. Steve's events at Crystal Palace necessitated installation of extra seating for capacity crowds, creating an 'electric' atmosphere. Steve became the outstanding successful British team manager, a role he undertook without payment and with much distinction.

One of the difficulties in the early days was that some local authorities would not allow karate in their premises. Durham was a good example – karate was not allowed in sports centres in this very large county. I wrote to the clerk of the council asking if I may be allowed to meet their committee representatives responsible for this policy, to put the case for karate and to answer any questions. The clerk responded promptly and I was given an appointment to meet the education sub-committee. I travelled by train, arriving in good time, mentally geared to 'present' to maybe six people – in my mind this would be a subcommittee – but I was surprised to be seated in front of over thirty members of the council. I was given a hard time and frankly thought I had 'lost'. However, the next morning I received the good news that the council had approved karate use of their sports facilities and so our official groups were able to move in. This was a big step forward, at the same time making it more difficult for the unofficial backstreet operators to compete.

The BKCC then produced the first brochure – 'The Misunderstood Sport'. This was widely circulated to councils and those with control of resources. The demand for instruction was such that sports centre operators soon found out that not only were karate-ka well disciplined but their numbers swelled the occupancy of their premises – good for the activity and the local finances.

Martial arts in general, and karate in particular, started to grow very quickly and some clubs trebled and quadrupled their membership. Our publicised successes in European and world competition also generated demand and the chapter on kung fu and Korean martial arts also describes parallel growth.

Cooperation among karate associations reached a peak by 1975. The major groups were constructively helping with stewarding, programme production, timekeeping, officials and local contacts. Our referees were now among the best in Europe. The climax of cooperation was possibly at the 1975 BKCC Championships at Belle Vue, Manchester, successfully sponsored by Greater Manchester Council and attracting a packed house. Normally the all-styles championships were held in October but this year they took place on 29 November due to the Long Beach, USA, October World Championships. The chief executive of the Greater Manchester Council and Deputy Chief Constable R S Barratt (later to become HM Chief Inspector of Constabulary and knighted) presented prizes, the event being followed by a buffet and social. It was a very good day and Ticky Donovan entered the Guinness Book of Records for his third consecutive win.

The only occasion I experienced some discourtesy was after I telephoned Len Palmer asking if I could address his association at their general meeting in Nottingham. I wished to explain to and inform his gathered club representatives about some important proposals. I could tell on the telephone that Len Palmer was not keen for me to speak, but I needed to do it – the BKA was the only group who had not been fully informed: the previous weekend the KUGB had given unanimous approval to the same propositions.

I drove to Nottingham for the 2.30 p.m. start, taking a seat at the side of the stage waiting to be called to speak. My 'slot', including questions, would take ten minutes or so but it was not my intention to speak then rush away: I was willing to quietly hear the BKA go about its democratic business. The time, however, dragged on, and on, until I realised that Len Palmer was going to try to exclude me from speaking on grounds of lack of time. The hall caretaker appeared, indicating that the meeting was overrunning and he wanted his hall vacated! At this stage I stood up and asked to speak. I addressed the meeting with their concurrence, said what I wished to say then asked for an indication of approval. The meeting approved. Len Palmer was not pleased and I pondered, possibly unkindly, while driving home that he might be the only disapproving individual in the whole membership. It was, after all, Len who had invited me into karate and I had no wish to argue with him. I telephoned the result to Bryn Williams after being home very much later than anticipated: another long Sunday.

Reverting to karate's overall expansion, such success and high demand also brings problems. Some very credible and respected instructors began to challenge the policy and the need to belong to a style organisation in order to stay within the BKCC. The

British Karate Association would normally be the 'all-styles' group for disaffected karate-ka to join, but this was not what defectors wanted. I tried hard to convince members that they should stay within their associations to influence by democratic means. A typical example was that of a major problem affecting the KUGB – looked upon as the largest and most efficient association.

The following open letter from Cliff Hepburn, KUGB secretary, published in early 1976, amply illustrates the problem:

> The Karate Union of Great Britain represents Shotokan style in this country and has played a leading role in developing karate technically and politically. Members of the KUGB are therefore puzzled to hear that without reference to the KUGB elected committee, a Japanese instructor has commenced to sell his own licence under the eventual heading of Shotokan Karate International (SKI) So strong was the reaction of the members that an extraordinary meeting of the KUGB was called. Over 152 clubs sent representatives ... The EGM heard Mr Shoji, Director of the JKA, Tokyo, state that the JKA would recognise only one Shotokan group in Great Britain and that was the KUGB. The President of European Shotokan sent a letter which was read to the meeting stating that one Great Britain Shotokan group was recognised: the KUGB.
>
> The chairman of the BKCC was invited to speak and declared that the BKCC constitution would allow only one group per style in membership of the BKCC. The recognised group was the KUGB. He urged potential SKI members not to fragment into another unconstitutional organisation but to stay with the KUGB and so automatically contribute to karate within the proper channels. Voting in support of KUGB policy was 126 to 26.

The Cliff Hepburn letter went on to say that the door would be kept open if any club wished to rejoin. Overall it was a good letter reflecting BKCC and KUGB policy but politics is not a stable science and there was more to this growing problem, some of it brought about by the huge growth in demand. There was also the increased technical ability of British instructors coupled with the growing expertise of smaller groups to run their own affairs without the need to join large groups. There were other 'declarations of independence': the Amateur Karate Association, led by Tom Hibbert, had evolved out of the UKKF, Thames Shotokan led by Ray and Pauline Fuller left the KUGB plus another very credible Shotokan group based in Picketts Lock, North London. Walter Seaton (originally 1st Dan Shotokan) led many Wado-Ryu ex-UKKF clubs in the North East and thrived with distinction as England Karate-do Wado-kai. Peter Spanton, an excellent athlete, leader and Wado Ryu instructor led a separate large group of ex-BKA clubs in the West Country where there was superb team spirit and high standards. Keith Morris, a university lecturer, and Albert Hampson, a school teacher, were leaders in Shotokan Karate International who wished to follow instructor Hirokasu Kanazawa (coach of the Japan national team).

I met Keinosuke Enoeda and Hirokasu Kanazawa in Soho. Clearly there was no possibility of getting together and there was no meal. I had seen Kanazawa in action at Nottingham University sports centre and witnessed the ecstatic reception of the audience and enthusiastic queue of followers awaiting his autograph. Both instructors were revered. I knew there could be no solution under BKCC member KUGB, though the KUGB had my sympathy in this dispute. One had to face reality – the SKI had credibility and was led by very responsible and likeable people.

I could not go along with the vociferous demands of some committee members – that we should arrange ejection from sports centres of those who had left their associations. The problem was not so easily solved as that. These technically good, established clubs had members who were taxpayers and ratepayers: one just cannot ask local sports centres to ban them on karate-political grounds. I had telephone calls at work (which I discouraged) and late night calls at home, some after midnight, demanding that I take strong action. 'We need to get control' was the theme by some members. I had to point out to them that if we were not careful we would be controlling less and less. Our responsibility was national and if possible national unity.

I finally visited all the major groups who had broken away to establish personally why and also how they saw their future. They were good people, we needed them in the main body but they were no longer prepared to contribute fees and time to the big style associations. Back at the BKCC it was showdown time. Something had to be done to prevent serious haemorrhage. I could no longer go along with the demands for ejection so I resigned the chair. I revisited five groups concerned who agreed without demur to join a 'Federation of English Karate Organisations' (FEKO) and then apply to join the BKCC. The FEKO meetings were held on Sundays in Nottingham – all the members were established players, technically and organisationally sound – and it was a pleasure to help them. However, though this event did not endear me to some BKCC groups it nevertheless reunited karate for the time being.

It was with FEKO – referring to the title of this book – that I 'dropped one of the balls'. At the time I had an interest in several bank accounts at the National Westminster Bank, first with manager Alan Mason and later Peter Hart with whom I still correspond every Christmas.

The bank accounts were British Karate Control Commission, Federation of English Karate Organisations, European Karate Union and Police Superintendents' Association of England and Wales. Each association within FEKO had agreed to subscribe £200 into the account which would give an immediate £1000 administration fund. I was handed £200 cash to pay in for one of the associations and, not wishing personally to carry this sum longer than necessary, used a back-of-the-book paying-in slip of the Superintendents' Association carefully crossing out all references and account numbers and substituting the FEKO name and account numbers. The age of electronic/magnetic banking had arrived and the £200 went straight into the busy Superintendents' Association account. When it came to the audit of the FEKO accounts I was chief suspect as the stated cash credit could not be found! Alan Mason, the bank manager, came to my rescue by finding the original altered slip in the bank's daily bundle and I learned lessons:

1.   Do not take shortcuts with others' money; and

2.   Keep up to date with new banking technology.

Returning to karate politics, there was a secondary reason for my resignation from BKCC. I had let it be known that I had no long-

36

term ambition to chair the BKCC, indeed two deputy chairmen had been appointed: Derek Langham of the KUGB and Major John Green of the UKKF, both very respected and capable of taking over if elected. Martial arts as such were experiencing major growth – very few sports centres nationally were without karate, kung fu or tae kwon do and the time had come to develop a new 'ten-year plan'. The Sports Council could not possibly deal with a proliferation of groups and for the good of the martial arts as a whole the best course was that a Martial Arts Commission be formed; one body to which all the groups could belong while retaining their own autonomy, karate obviously being the major group with the most experience.[*]

This suggestion, originally promulgated and supported by the BKCC also received the support of Denis Howell, the Minister of Sport and he duly attended Wood Street police station to announce to the press and all invited bodies that a Martial Arts Commission (MAC) would receive official recognition. He praised the BKCC for enabling and encouraging this to come about. The minister was also the Member of Parliament for Birmingham and he asked the highly respected retiring Chief Constable of Birmingham, Sir Derek Capper, if he would accept a nomination for the Chair of the Martial Arts Commission. This duly came about.

In the spring of 1976, soon after England had won the European Karate Championship in Teheran, Bryn Williams successfully responded to a national advertisement for the position of Director of Administration (subsequently Director of Youth Development and Coaching) with Jimmy Hill's 'World Sports Academy', contracted to organise football in Saudi Arabia, a wonderful opportunity.

Sir Derek Capper's and Bryn Williams' next priority was to seek and appoint a new general secretary for the Martial Arts Commission. Interviews were conducted and David Mitchell of the BKA, highly qualified academically and in karate, was appointed.

The MAC took over the offices of the BKCC at 4–6 Deptford Bridge, Deptford, London. These offices were rented from City

---

[*] In 2007, the number of groups had totalled 232.

solicitors Stafford Clark and Co (later Stafford Young Jones) established for over 100 years in the City of London. They had also been instrumental in obtaining the Martini Terrace in New Zealand House for several BKCC receptions, a valuable connection via a senior partner.

Alas, after the official launch of the MAC in the Martini Terrace Sir Derek Capper died from a heart attack and MAC was never to feel the benefit and wisdom of this one-time athlete and chief constable; a great loss. David Mitchell and I attended his memorial service at St Martin's Church in the Bull Ring, Birmingham, together with Jim Elkin of the British Aikido Association, who was to take over as chairman of MAC. Most police forces nationally were represented and we took lunch in Birmingham Police Headquarters. It was a sad day.

There was a lot of work to be done. Jim Elkin, a genial man with an exceptional war record in the Royal Navy (Battle of the River Plate) sincerely gave his best but he did not have time to succeed before he, too, died suddenly. This was also a great loss to martial arts.

By this time I was becoming remote from the scene and working for Mecca Leisure. I had stepped back from most of the sports activity which had not only consumed so much time and many weekends, but had encompassed enriching experiences and friendships during eight years of intensive activity. I also needed to give overdue attention to home and growing family with which my wife had so competently coped.

Eight years – 'two terms' in political life – was enough. It was time for others to carry on with fresh ideas and fresh energy.

The British Kung Fu Council

Origin

The BKCC member associations were surprised by the surge in growth of kung fu and the immense publicity for Chinese martial arts achieved in the 1970s. David Carradine featured in a popular television *Kung Fu* series every Sunday, Bruce Lee films were a huge success, James Bond films featured scenes with martial arts schools and some extraordinary self-defence feats. At the height of the publicity, the *Daily Mirror*, for example, ran a double page spread headed 'Kungfumania', and in the high streets glossy magazine shelves brimmed with kung fu articles and features. This combination caused the demand for kung fu to far exceed the supply of available instructors, and some unscrupulous operators exploited this market. At one point, Bryn Williams received three sacks of letters in one week, asking for addresses of karate and kung fu/wu shu clubs, which he redistributed to locally recognised organisations.

At this time, the Republic of China sent a large martial arts group called 'Wu Shu' to London. They gave skilful demonstrations, being very fit, flexible athletes and 'tumblers'. Prior to these exhibitions in major public venues, a reception was held at the Embassy of China, to which Bryn Williams and I were invited. The excellent publicity Wu Shu attracted created even more demand for kung fu and martial arts in general.

Advertisements, placed mainly by UK nationals, then appeared in the local press on these lines:

> Learn Kung Fu. You've seen it on TV, now try it for yourself. Beginners welcome. Buy your kit and get started. Come to the Church Hall [address] on [date and time]. Sign up. Learn from the experts.

All was not well with some of these advertisements, and students' money was at risk. The modus operandi would be as follows:

First, a brief demonstration by instructors (possibly versed in karate but switching to 'kung fu'), followed by a plausible talk on the quality and genuine origins of their 'style'. Fees for courses would be collected, kits would be sold and the classes would begin. For example, if a course cost £35 and a kit £25, then one hundred students, signing up, would produce a substantial income after costs. Several of these venues could produce a large turnover, inevitably evading the national tax system in the process.

Then comes the problem: the operators will say that the church authority (for example) does not like the activity and demands it ceases. The truth is more likely to be that the operators have not fully paid next month's rent and the agreement is cancelled. The advertisers in the north could operate from an address in the south, and vice versa.

Complaints were received by local karate organisations and the BKCC, so it was agreed to take action, despite our karate brief not extending to kung fu. The BKCC association members were unanimous for decisive action and guidance. It was required we should take the lead, and Bryn and I were charged by the BKCC with the task of producing results.

Through magazine and directory lists, genuine kung fu organisations were contacted directly by letter from the Sports Council or indirectly by publicity. A meeting was called. The British Kung Fu Council (BKFC) evolved from this on the same lines as the BKCC, and from this meeting the founder members elected a small technical committee to assess the competence of applicants, and indeed to demonstrate to each other their own abilities. A constitution and code of conduct was produced for approval and adoption and the Council was 'operational' with a lot of goodwill in very quick time. It meant a lot more visiting of clubs, and we were keen to embrace members of the Chinese community, where there was much talent. Bryn and I ate at Chinese restaurants in all sorts of locations, and the Chinese seemed well pleased at the prospect of official recognition. Some restaurants would not accept money for the meals, as word went round that we were there to help, in which case we tipped heavily to keep our credibility.

Meanwhile our wives at home needed even more patience, as we returned home late with detectable traces of having enjoyed Chinese food. Another busy day at the office...

The kung fu operators, with one exception which I shall describe later, were much more relaxed at committee than the karate representatives. The first assessment meetings and technical tests were held in a hotel at Junction 2 of the M6. (It was then called the 'Coventry Esso Hotel' and later became a Crest Hotel.) This venue was ideal for the purpose, with three large main function rooms of equal size: one for the applicants to change; one for the applicants to relax, warm up and rehearse; and one for the BKFC Technical Committee and vetting group to assess the demonstration and ask questions. Unexpectedly, the candidates insisted on showing their power by breaking bricks, paving and wood. We told them there was no need, but they had come prepared to do it and wished to proceed. The hotel manager had never seen anything like it and ordered a skip to clear the debris – a new experience for him! Another vetting weekend or two went by, and it was valuable work to achieve the objective. Applicants came from all over the country, including Scotland, to undertake the tests seriously and with goodwill, all to obtain recognition. Groups with Hong Kong and Malaysian origins also joined and gave demonstrations of their technical ability.

The benefit of joining the new body was recognition on the same lines as membership of the BKCC, giving access to official sports premises, which were an increasing feature in many towns. The indirect benefits to the BKCC were that activities of competitive substandard operators were curtailed, or at least made more difficult.

A typical example of successful sports centre access was a group led by Tony Leung, originally Hong Kong based, but now with a club in King's Cross and another in Southwark near London Bridge Station. He successfully opened up in Orpington and did very well.

The publication called *The Ugly Shadow* was designed by ace photographer Robert Hope of the *Daily Telegraph* (he had also designed City of London Police recruiting brochures). It carried a foreword from Denis Howell, the Minister for Sport, with pictures of the BKCC and the BKFC committees. A shadow appearing from a suspect advertisement alerted members of the public, local authorities and those with resources to deal only with members of recognised governing bodies. The publication had much impact, being widely distributed to local authorities, church premises, libraries and sports centres, as operators of facilities soon realised they also had responsibilities for control.

Hyde Park Jubilee Celebrations

In 1977, HM The Queen celebrated her Silver Jubilee and celebrations included cultural and sporting activities across the country. At the Hyde Park event in London, the British Kung Fu Council arranged a demonstration which was visited by HRH Princess Alexandra. There was also a dragon dance, and the kung fu participants, mainly Soho and West End Chinese waiters, were introduced. It was a very successful occasion watched by a large crowd and the Chinese were delighted.

There used to be a large 'Corner House' in Coventry Street, London, operated by J Lyons and Co. On a Boxing Day, when Soho restaurants virtually shut down, Mary and I were invited to the 'Corner House', now a huge Chinese restaurant, to witness a relaxed afternoon of martial arts demonstrations and dragon dance performed by the off-duty waiters, of which there were several hundred. Jim Elkin of the British Aikido Association was also invited with his wife. As the only Europeans there, we felt privileged to be at this memorable and happy occasion, followed by a meal. Having been frequent customers in the original 'Lyons Corner House' days, we were surprised and appreciative of the transformation, decor and activity in addition to the hospitality.

Discipline Problems

I now return to the earlier indication that there was an exception to normal and expected courtesy, an incident which justified disciplinary action. The members of the officially recognised martial arts bodies combined to stage an evening of martial arts at

Crystal Palace National Sports Centre in aid of funds for the Prince's Trust. All sports governing bodies had been requested to participate by Arthur Rees, Chairman of the Prince's Trust fund-raising group. Mr Rees, a wartime fighter pilot (Mustangs), was once a distinguished Wales and Cambridge University rugby international, playing when Wales beat the All Blacks. This much-respected retired Chief Constable of Staffordshire was guest of honour to witness the Crystal Palace charity event, and the sell-out evening was very successful. Karate, aikido, kendo, tae kwon do and kung fu groups participated.

During a kung fu demonstration, a small section of the audience, belonging to a non-Chinese kung fu group, but within membership of the British Kung Fu Council, behaved badly by calling out derisory remarks at the participants. It was mainly unnoticed by the public, but to martial arts practitioners it was very disrespectful. This group – its leader among them – was promptly suspended and told to expect disciplinary action.

The next meeting of the British Kung Fu Council was held one month later in Birmingham. I travelled there on a Sunday with Tony McCarthy, a member of the BKFC executive committee, and programme producer on ITV's *World of Sport*, a very popular sports programme, broadcasting on Saturday afternoons. I had worked for his father, a City of London police inspector. The meeting of the Council, which I chaired, took place in a fourth-floor room of a hotel in New Street, and was well under way when about ten members of the suspended London group, with their European leader, unexpectedly arrived demanding to be heard, protesting loudly about their suspension.

It was immediately obvious they were about to cause trouble, and I could sense that violence was possible, almost imminent. I stopped the meeting and members stood up. The atmosphere was now electric. Police had been sent for by the hotel. I stood on a chair and announced to all concerned that there must be no violence. 'The first person to raise a fist in here will later face the full consequences!' I heard myself say. I was conscious of the fact we were on the fourth floor and the windows were open! Any violence here would make newspaper and television headlines, setting back the good name of martial arts for years, and providing a gift story for the tabloids. A lone policeman arrived. With hindsight I could see the funny side. Here, in a room full of men skilled in fighting arts, one police officer stood no chance, had anyone lost his head and struck the first blow! I mused on a possible collective noun for fighting martial artists.

The interlopers left. There was no violence and we then called for tea to refresh and resettle. As I drank tea I used both hands on the cup, with elbows on the table, to hide the fact that my hands might be shaking. I thought about what the family at home were doing, about the fact I was absent for yet another Sunday, but it was all 'in the interest of progress'. I had seen this miscreant group giving a demonstration in a large South London theatre and knew they were formidable. They stayed suspended, their actions compounded by this new appalling behaviour, to be firmly dealt with another day. It was the only potentially serious event during my close involvement with martial arts.

Soho Chinese Community

However, I did become involved following an incident where two senior Chinese kung fu instructors, much respected in Soho, where they taught student classes, had been arrested and charged with assault on police. The respected proprietor of a well-known Chinese restaurant telephoned and asked to see me, requesting advice. This was unusual, and I was pleased to meet him in my office at Wood Street.

He declared that the two accused kung fu instructors were in their car in Croydon, waiting at traffic lights, when another car with two men pulled alongside, gesticulating forcefully that they were going to cut in front. The two Chinese remonstrated at what they thought was selfish behaviour, whereupon the occupants of the second car got out and threatened them. There was a general altercation and scuffle, resulting in the Chinese, much to their surprise, being arrested for assault on police. No one had been injured. One of the Chinese had made the mistake of getting out of his car with a starting handle, but there was no charge of 'offensive weapon'.

It was suggested that a police prosecution could result in a gross injustice, causing loss of face for the accused. Their whole philosophy in kung fu teaching was non-aggression, so a conviction for assault on police would be very damaging. I agreed to meet the two waiters, circumspect about getting too involved with an incident in the Metropolitan Police area. I suggested to the two Chinese that if they had indeed assaulted police, as alleged, then the best course of action would be to plead guilty at the magistrates' court, getting a lawyer to put mitigating circumstances. They both, with strong eye contact, solemnly and vehemently denied the police allegation. I advised them to seek the advice of a lawyer, plead not guilty, and ask for trial at a Crown court. If desired, I would attend to give evidence that they were members of the officially recognised governing body for kung fu, that their stance was non-aggression, and that they had the capability and knowledge to inflict physical damage – which they had not done, indicating restraint. After committal by Croydon Magistrates, the trial took place at Croydon Crown Court and I was called to give evidence.

The police, originally in plain clothes, wore uniform at court, which I thought would unfairly influence the jury. After a very short deliberation by the jury, both waiters were found not guilty and discharged. I did not speak to the police and there was no celebration by the defence. It was not a happy day, but justice had been done and it was their right to receive a fair hearing. I was at peace with the outcome and their good name in Soho was preserved.

The 'Soho connection' with the Chinese community I remember with affection, and thirty years on I still attend the award-winning Fung Shing restaurant in Lisle Street with family and friends.

Kung Fu Flails

In mid-1977, the City of London police arrested a team of known robbers who were stationary in their motor car. It was thought the suspects were waiting to ambush a City bank cash delivery, which was in accord with the undercover information received. Checks revealed they had previous convictions for violent robbery, but the actual evidence for this current event was thin. It had been a difficult decision for police, whether to arrest during the attack, in which case someone might have been severely injured, or arrest before the attack, hoping for extra evidence such as masks, et cetera. In the car were rice flails, known as 'kung fu flails' (two pieces of wood joined by chain and popularised by Bruce Lee) or 'nunchaku' (a Japanese version joined by cord). I was asked about them, the key question being: were the flails made to be offensive, or did intention to use offensively have to be proved? Our flour now comes in bags and we do not need to flail crops to separate the husks. If the carrier of a rice flail is a member of a bona fide martial arts club and on way to training, for example, this would be an excellent defence; but to be outside a bank in the middle of the day with rice flails would stretch the imagination of the most patient jury. This was one of the rare instances in law where the onus of proof – here of lawful use – shifts to the accused.

I attended Guildhall Magistrates' Court to give evidence that in my opinion the weapons were, in the absence of any plausible explanation to the contrary, made to be offensive. Not only could the rice flail break two upright bricks when swung at speed, it could also fracture a skull or bring about death in seconds by shutting off the carotid artery blood supply to the brain. If the chain or cord was swung round the neck, it could be used as a lever to produce pressure simultaneously on both arteries. The magistrates accepted the prosecution case, but only after a lot of discussion. The defence did not appeal.

Following this case, I wrote an article for the *Police Review*, a national newspaper widely read by police, drawing attention to the problem of rice flails. Some police readers, who were having difficulty with their prosecutions, requested I give advice and evidence. The year was 1978, and I was now working for Mecca Leisure as Group Security Adviser. I explained to the company that this activity was a helpful public service and the Chairman, Michael Guthrie (who would have made a good Chief Constable), agreed to the request that I assist police. Not all the cases were straightforward, because rice flails were new to magistrates, judges and juries. Some were reluctant to convict if they were not sure: their prerogative.

In the next year or two I gave evidence in Dover, Gravesend, Dartford, Middlesex Guildhall, Harlow, Preston Crown Court and at Leyland, Lancashire. Travel costs were claimed from the courts. Mecca Leisure also published rice flail advice for the door supervisors in their numerous discos and dance halls, advising the then London County Council on rules of conduct for door supervisors. 'Disco Rules OK!' was duly published by the LCC. A group of LCC councillors also visited several major Mecca branches to see dance operations and door supervisors at work. The martial arts press cooperated by publishing BKCC and BKFC advice that flails used in training should be wrapped in kit or a towel and kept in a sports bag whilst travelling – and positively no training whilst waiting at a bus stop!

Soon after leaving the police service to join Mecca Leisure, I left the chair of the BKFC, the meetings continuing in hotels. Travelling the country for Mecca Leisure, with approximately 250 branches nationwide, and this new role to master, allowed no more time to spare, so I handed the reins to others. I had much enjoyed my BKFC association and the loyal support from members.

The British Association of Korean Martial Arts (BAKMA)

Rhee Ki Ha, 7th dan and leader of the United Kingdom Tae kwon do Association (UKTA), hearing of BKCC activity before publication of *The Ugly Shadow*, contacted Bryn Williams at the office of the BKCC, asking for a meeting. The UKTA was well established, had much credibility, and Rhee Ki Ha was a well-known and respected practitioner. The International Tae kwon do Federation was founded by General Choi Hong Hi, President, based in Canada. Bryn Williams and I duly met Rhee Ki Ha in the Serpentine Restaurant at Hyde Park, where we had a good discussion. The event was reported to the BKCC, and the UKTA was specifically mentioned in *The Ugly Shadow* as a group with which we cooperated.

I was present at Claridges Hotel when His Excellency the Ambassador of Korea awarded Rhee Ki Ha with the Order of Civil Merit, a gold medal, on behalf of the Korean Government for his development of Tae kwon do internationally, a very happy occasion.

The publication of *The Ugly Shadow* had considerable impact. No less than three organisations calling themselves 'British Tae kwon do Association' made contact with Bryn Williams at the BKCC offices. There were also Kup Sool and Hap Ki-do groups, who had technical credibility.

We also declared these events to the BKCC Committee and then went ahead with another inaugural meeting, Sports Council backed, to form the British Association of Korean Martial Arts. With Bryn as secretary, meetings were held on weekday evenings at Wood Street police station. The three British Tae kwon do Associations merged into one group for the purposes of coming together in BAKMA. This was progress. Bryn and I were very impressed with the committee of BAKMA; most had university backgrounds and degrees and they talked sense. Of all the groups and meetings, this was the one with the potential and capability to make fast progress.

A dramatic twist then occurred. In Korea there was a change of political leadership and Rhee Ki Ha and the UKTA were suddenly no longer recognised by the Korean Government as the official Tae kwon do organisation; this recognition was now to be vested in the British Tae kwon do Association, and letters followed confirming this. I felt sorry for the members of the UKTA, British citizens paying local rates and national taxes. Suddenly, through no fault of their own, their tae kwon do organisation is outside the internationally recognised body. One cannot swim long-term against the tide and survive, so the situation had to be accepted.

Korea was pushing to get tae kwon do into the Olympics and, much to their credit, was ultimately successful, well ahead of karate, which has yet to achieve this status. The UKTA continued to do well, running their own courses and international matches; indeed, they were of the highest international standard. Having won their World Tae kwon do Championship, Mecca Leisure sponsored a UKTA celebration buffet lunch in the City of London, and the victorious team attended. The UKTA was well capable of filling the Crystal Palace National Sports Centre, and duly did so on the occasion I attended, there being no empty seats.

In 1977 the now officially recognised Tae kwon do World Championships were to be held in Chicago, USA. I saw Eric Morley at another 8 a.m Mecca Head Office Saturday meeting when he agreed to sponsor some air fares in support of the British team. Using this help, I was able to go to the championships, attend the Congress and enjoy the meetings and American hospitality at the Chicago Hilton. The event was well organised, and the hotel for the British Team and officials was near to the sports arena for the championships. Unfortunately, I left open my fifth floor hotel room balcony sliding door, so when I returned late after a very long day I found the carpet damp from a thunderstorm. Next morning, dozens of mushrooms had grown overnight on the carpet – extraordinary!

The British team members, managed by barrister Freddie Lee, 6th dan, acquitted themselves well, but were no match against more established and experienced practitioners, for example American and Korean nationals. I had been so busy at meetings in Chicago that I had not seen the town and had been unable to fulfil my intention of informally presenting a City of London Police shield to the Chicago Police. To correct this, I got up very early to embark on an intensive fast walk, to enjoy a dawn view of Lake Michigan and generally view the skyscrapers. I was displeased when leaving the hotel at 5 a.m. to see several members of the British team coming in for bed! (The transport for the airport was due at 9 a.m. Had anyone been late for that, I would have been disapproving, but the coach departed promptly with all aboard. I felt karate athletes would have been more disciplined.)

Chicago Police were very mobile; patrolling cars cruised slowly around, even at that time of the morning, and the town seemed well policed. Standing on any corner, it seemed to me that one was bound to see a patrol car. Having taken the city shield with me, I stopped one of the cars, had a good talk with the crew, asking them to accept the shield for their station with my compliments and apologies for the style of presentation. They appreciated the shield and I enjoyed the interlude in the fresh morning air. At the police station only the cleaners, not the Superintendent, would have been about at that early hour!

I was amused at one Chicago hostel for 'down and outs' and drunks. Whilst they waited for attention under a canopy in the street, gospel music and sermons played continuously. I hope they appreciated it, but I have doubts.

I interfered somewhat with the proposed return travel arrangements. Having travelled alone to Chicago by British Airways flight, I was unaware of the route of travel of the team and officials who were already there. On enquiring about the return route I was surprised to be told the team was flying Aer Lingus to Shannon and then by domestic flight to London. I asked why and arrived at the truth: the supporting Koreans in the party were nervous about flying into Heathrow direct because of immigration controls. By flying to Shannon and then coming to London by local Aer Lingus they anticipated less potential trouble! I was instrumental in switching the team to a British Airways flight direct from Chicago to Heathrow to face the proper passport controls openly. A British team should proudly come home via the front door. There was no problem, and in any case I had the annual conference of the Police Superintendents' Association of England and Wales (of which I was honorary treasurer) due at Eastbourne, so I had no wish to delay by flying via Shannon. I was tired when I presented the accounts, but they had been professionally and thoroughly audited!

I had been asked to be a vice president of the World Tae kwon do Association but declined with respectful thanks, as my first loves were judo and karate, and I did not wish to feel unduly obligated to tae kwon do. However I was grateful for the offer, especially as major events in Korea, including the Olympics, were being planned. I had a lot of work to do and felt that I must leave Korea to others.

I duly reported back to Eric Morley, with grateful thanks from all concerned in the British Tae kwon do team.

In 2007 Rhee Ki Ha, passing through London, kindly telephoned me at home – over thirty years on – and it was a pleasure to hear from him.

As I write this, the next Olympic Games are due to take place in Beijing and London, at which Great Britain will enter tae kwon do teams. Karate has been unsuccessful in achieving this status. We have many years' experience since the early mid-1970 days and we wish the teams and individuals every success. Great Britain was the first national team to beat Japan at karate in 1972, and we hope Beijing in 2008 and London in 2012 will be opportunities to show similar success in tae kwon do against strong Koreans and the other nations.

The European Scene

Bryn Williams and I were mandated by the BKCC to be the representatives for Great Britain at the 1970 European Union of Karate meeting in Paris. We duly introduced ourselves to Jacques Delcourt, a lawyer and President of the French Karate Federation and European Karate Union (EKU). He was very much in charge of all things karate in France and Europe. I believe he was at first wary of Bryn and me because the BKCC had major Japanese-led associations in membership, and Delcourt wished to avoid Japanese political and financial influence, unaware at that time where the BKCC stood. At the EKU Congress, Delcourt made a speech of welcome in English. To his credit he had spent time on quotations and started to recite from the well-known Kipling poem, 'If'. It so happened I carried this poem in my briefcase to reread in spare moments, and I waved it to him in support of what he was saying. I later gave him the copy, and he very much appreciated it, this interaction having been well received by the delegates. As time progressed we got on very well and I came to like his style.

Jacques Delcourt was particularly pleased that I had obtained a top-quality English translation of the statutes of the European Karate Union, hitherto only available in French. This skilled translation was produced at no cost, save a bottle of single malt, by a linguist at the Moscow Narodny Bank in Cannon Street. It was very helpful to the European countries.

The French were good hosts at the Paris European Championships, and all the competitors, officials and delegates were taken on a guided tour of the Hôtel de Ville (Town Hall) in Paris. The decor and painted ceilings were superb, and I was relieved that they had survived the war.

Jacques Delcourt was very sensitive about international karate-style championships being staged in Europe. He wanted all-styles championships only, at which everyone stood a chance of being selected. Bryn Williams and I counselled him that separate-style-only championships (such as shotokan and wado-ryu) could do no harm; they were not a challenge, so why politically fight against them? The main championship that mattered was the European Karate Union all-style championship, to which all the recognised governing bodies sent their best teams. The BKCC represented all styles, so what was the problem? He considered our point and I think he relaxed.

On the home front, these style championships gave our competitors a lot of experience. First, competitors had their own association's competitions, then the BKCC championships, and finally national team elimination contests. Compare the situation in America, for example, where cross-country competitions would involve huge expense, up to four time zones and loss of time in travel: here in Britain we were mobile, and karateka were enthusiastic competitors, with ease of motorway and train travel. It was an immense advantage to train and compete in Great Britain.

Fanfare for Europe

In November 1972 the BKCC was accorded a great honour by the Government, being asked by Lord Mancroft to participate in celebrations for entering the European Economic Community in 1973. 'Fanfare for Europe' was arranging a week of cultural and sporting activities with European countries, commencing with football, England v Italy at Wembley Stadium, and concluding with karate, Great Britain v France at Crystal Palace on Saturday, 13 January 1973. Bryn Williams had done most of the background work to achieve this, and just before Christmas 1972 I flew to Paris to see Jacques Delcourt to go over proposed arrangements, emphasise the importance of this event and to increase the number of competitors in each team. The French were basking in the glory of being 1972 World Champions and the Great Britain team was similarly highly respected, having beaten Japan in the same 1972 Paris championships.

My critical trip to see Jacques Delcourt was nearly abandoned due to fog in Paris, but British Trident planes were specially equipped to cope with this. Looking out of the aircraft at what I thought was thick cloud, I was suddenly shocked to see the runway several metres below, followed by the landing. The Paris meeting was swift and very successful and I was back at my desk in Wood Street by 4 p.m., to find the City beginning to wind down for Christmas. In Paris we had agreed the team numbers, method and route of travel, the referee (Hugh Thompson from South Africa – he had been outstanding at the 1972 Paris World Championships), the judges, hotel accommodation and the format of the competition. Having done that it was back to focusing on the beloved City.

The night of 13 February 1973 was memorable. Crystal Palace National Sports Centre was crowded to capacity, all seats having to be numbered and ticket-allocated. Anticipation was high and all the BKCC associations cooperated closely to provide supporting demonstrations, stewarding and general backup. There was a reception on the balcony for VIPs and we all dressed in 'uniform' – blazers, grey flannels with white shirts, and BKCC ties. A Bromley school provided senior girls in school uniform to sell programmes and we were all on 'best behaviour'. The Fanfare for Europe committee was sponsoring the event, and our principal guests included Dr Sir Roger and Lady Bannister of the Sports Council, The Rt. Hon. Lord Sandford, of the Department of the Environment, and a senior secretary from the Embassy of France. Miss Jenny McAdam, Miss United Kingdom, arrived to distribute the new EEC minted crown coins to competitors and officials. The teams were then led by two thirteen-year-old youths: Timothy May, son of Dr Roger May (previously medical officer to BKCC), brought in the Great Britain team, and my son, Paul Francis, simultaneously led in the French team, each carrying the team's respective national flag. It had been rehearsed – without the competitors – to the music of Richard Strauss's *2001: A Space Odyssey* and later, as the teams unfolded into their positions facing each other, the timing was perfect. The music was the idea of Mary Williams – very successful – and has since been imitated by others.

Though Great Britain was marginally losing at the conclusion of the first round, the team, captained by Terry O'Neill of the KUGB, came back strongly against France in the second round to win the Fanfare for Europe trophy. It was a great night for karate and Great Britain in particular. Also present at the event was Geoffrey Gass, of the City and Metropolitan Building Society, fellow commuter and Chairman-elect of the City of London Police Committee. He gave pride of place to the Fanfare for Europe trophy, with pictures, in the building society's prime window site in Ludgate Hill, City of London, to be seen by thousands daily. Later the trophy was displayed in clubs round the country, unfortunately disappearing in the process.

On another occasion, Bryn Williams and I flew to Paris, accompanied by Steve Arneil, who had been asked by the French Federation to referee a France v Sweden karate match. Bryn and I were there to attend the European Karate Union (EKU) Committee meeting (at which Bryn was asked to become treasurer of the EKU, an honour which indicated their growing confidence in the BKCC). In the evening we attended the Sweden v France match at the packed Pierre de Coubertin Stadium, where Steve Arneil was an outstanding referee. Next afternoon we tried to fly back to Heathrow, but alas, there was an unexpected French air traffic controllers' strike, grounding all planes. The only way to get back to London was to catch the night ferry from Calais to Dover.

It was essential to be back at work before 9 a.m. on the Monday. Lateness is frowned upon in the police service. There is a canteen-humour culture to go with it, and I had no wish to become part of it. One City magistrate, who was invariably late for court, keeping everyone waiting, was always known as 'the late Sir Denys' and a constable, twice late in one week due to trains, was promptly nicknamed 'Silas' (Sorry I'm Late Again, Sergeant)!

So we talked through the evening in a Paris café, alternating coffee with beer and sandwiches, to await the 9 p.m. night ferry train from Paris Gare du Nord. The ship *Dunkerque Ferry* was uncomfortable and crowded. We arrived in Dover at 6.30 and then to Wood Street at 8.30 a.m.; by then we'd been talking all night and I had cut myself shaving in the shaking confines of the train toilet. It was not until four o'clock in the afternoon that I began to feel the effects of all this, necessitating a sound sleep that night. Another very long weekend away from home…

On several occasions at the Pierre de Coubertin Stadium in Paris we had watched proceedings carefully, for Great Britain was to host the 1974 European Championship at Crystal Palace National Sports Centre. We noted that there was no air conditioning in the Paris Stadium, and the atmosphere could be hot and sticky. Also the teams had no easy way of getting refreshment, making a very long day at this venue. There was no such poor air problem at Crystal Palace National Sports Centre, and we resolved that, out of the expected substantial revenue, we would provide all competitors with airline-style lunch 'flight packs'. In the event at Crystal Palace, this was so popular with the competitors that we were embarrassingly applauded when walking in front of the teams in the terraced seating. It was nice to be so genuinely and surprisingly thanked.

Through a long family friendship with a glass manufacturer, Harold Bruce (Parachute Regiment and Arnhem), we purchased one-pint glass beer jugs at cost, on which was engraved 'EUK 1974' – these also were very well received by all competitors and delegates. (The pint is now under threat from the litre!) Brian Hammond, our treasurer, had also provided kitbags suitably inscribed.

At earlier European Judo Championships at Crystal Palace, which I had attended by invitation from the British Judo Association, the band of the Grenadier Guards played to a packed audience and received a standing ovation as they marched off. I was very impressed. At Wood Street police station there were two colleagues of much public-spirited ability: Constable John Roach, ex-Pipe Major of the Irish Guards, and Detective Inspector John Langridge, ex-Drill Sergeant of the Coldstream Guards. They combined to train the City of London Girl Pipers. These girl pipers were superb – they played at major events like the Lord Mayors' Shows and the annual parade of the City of London Police Special Constabulary. They also toured in Great Britain and Europe. I asked if they would play at the European Karate Championships and they were delighted to do so. The audience saw the Irish pipes and the counter-marching and it made a wonderful start for the event. They even had more scope than the Grenadier Guards, as the Guards could not march on the judo mats, whereas the City of London Girl Pipers could march and counter-march across the whole Crystal Palace wood floor.

Another hat I wore was that of Chairman of the City of London Police Athletic Club. The secretary, Sergeant Tony Armfield, had completed a stocktake of all accumulated police trophies, some very old, so old in fact that their origins had been lost in time, but the quality remained. They were taking up space in cupboards and had to be cleaned. So we got approval to sell a number of these trophies. I went to John Fox, the public relations officer at Whitbread's Brewery at the north of the City, where we then kept our police horses, asking if they would like to sponsor a trophy in the European Karate Championships. They agreed. (I knew Whitbread's well, because as a constable I used to attend the brewery on Tuesday evenings to teach judo to their apprentices.) Likewise I saw Derek Ufton, Sport Liaison Executive at the Mecca Sportsman, who sponsored another trophy. The BKCC bought a trophy and the City of London Police Athletic Club donated the fourth. All these trophies were 'dipped', polished and re-engraved, and all concerned were pleased; a good example of quality recycling.

A European championship needs a lot of medals for individuals in weight categories and team contests, in gold, silver and bronze. The BKCC already had an established motif for the reverse of the medal, but the question arose, what goes on the prime obverse side of the medal? We were looking for a London connection. I went to see the General Purposes Committee Clerk in Guildhall, who obtained permission from the Chairman to use the coat of arms of the City of London. All the medals were then cast – gold, silver and bronze – and all delegates, winning competitors and officials were given a quality product in snap-to lidded case.

Next we needed a hotel with suitable accommodation for the 'Congress', a reception room and a room for a quality buffet. I knew the Tower Hotel near Tower Bridge could fulfil this triple requirement, so I went to see Richard Johnston, the Tower Hotel security officer (ex-Flying Squad, New Scotland Yard and ex-Pathfinder, Royal Air Force). Before long, everything was arranged, and the hotel was outstanding both in location and facilities.

Bryn's wife, Mary Williams, in evening dress, gave superb service to the Congress by acting as verbatim interpreter in English, French and Spanish; a very talented lady. It was at this Congress that we also got unanimous approval from the delegates that England, Scotland and Wales could each henceforth send delegates, enter competitions and act independently in Europe – a big breakthrough. Hitherto we could only enter two teams – England and Scotland – and one pair of delegates. Now we could further broaden our experience in competition and representation.

The British Karate Association, and secretary Len Palmer in particular, did not like the fact that Bryn Williams and I had caused his BKA chairman, Jeff Somers, to stand down from the EUK executive. Len knew we were mandated to do this as the new governing body for British karate, but Jeff Somers represented the BKA only, not the BKCC. I am sorry to say that from then on Len's support appeared to be passive compared with other members who contributed fully. I was sorry about this.

When in 1976 Bryn Williams announced he was going to help develop football in Saudi Arabia, leaving a vacancy for treasurer of the EKU, the EKU Committee asked that, for the time being, I take over this role to keep matters simple and to save moving bank accounts. This was the most difficult treasurership I had undertaken. Used to double-entry bookkeeping, in which I had been trained as a youngster, I could not make the EKU books balance due to the fluctuating pound, the dollar and the European currencies. Converting dollars, marks and francs into sterling and back was a problem, and I suddenly had more respect for international accountants! I simply listed all the transactions. All was checkable and no money was lost, so all concerned seemed happy – much to my relief. No 'balls had fallen' over Europe...

Bryn left soon after England had won the 1976 European Karate Championship in Teheran. It was at the peak time of our karate performances. He had made a major contribution to the EKU and BKCC and all concerned were very grateful. He was publicly thanked by Sir Derek Capper at a Martini Terrace reception at New Zealand House. David Mitchell was introduced at the same reception and became General Secretary of the new Martial Arts Commission. (Also see 'BKCC Origins and Development'.)

The 2nd World Karate Championships, Paris 1972

The Paris 1972 World Championships were held over the weekend of 21 and 22 April. Prior to this there was the Congress of the World Union of Karate-do Organisations (WUKO), at which Bryn Williams and I represented Great Britain.

The Japanese officials and senior supporters, on their way to France, arrived in London earlier in the week, and through the good offices of a senior partner of Stafford Clark and Co., solicitors in the City of London, we held a reception in the Martini Terrace at New Zealand House, overlooking Nelson's Column and Trafalgar Square. The reception for the Japanese included the Great Britain team and officials, key supporters, and was visited by Dr Sir Roger Bannister, Chairman of the Sports Council, who talked to the team, wishing them good luck. This reception promoted a lot of general goodwill and everyone was impressed with the panoramic view of London from the top of New Zealand House.

Brian Hammond, our treasurer, made the Paris travel arrangements for the British party and we had the exclusive use of the appropriately named Westminster Hotel near the Paris Opera House in the centre of the city.

At the Congress, we could tell Jacques Delcourt was still wary of Japanese political interference and potential financial domination, but this eased as time progressed. The European Karate Union had weaknesses, and refereeing experience was one of them. It was realised that the heavy programme of contests, needing six officials for each of three match areas, would produce demands during the weekend that could not be met by existing numbers of qualified referees. We just had to enlist the help of Japanese expertise. I pointed out that this would put a responsibility on the Japanese to show absolute impartiality and to fail to take advantage of this expertise when they would be on site would be foolhardy. This was accepted, and Keinosuke Enoeda and

Tatsuo Suzuki from Great Britain, with other senior well-known Japanese karateka, subsequently refereed well. As each year progressed, the refereeing ability of EKU and WUKO countries increased considerably, so, by the time of the 3rd World Championships three years later, refereeing shortages were not a problem.

This 1972 Congress was held in a frugally furnished military briefing room, which, considering the fact that delegates had travelled across the world, was rather hard. I sensed that Jacques Delcourt, a very capable lawyer and chairman, did not wish the meeting to last very long. Indeed, after the basic agenda had been completed and it was getting dark outside, he started to personally turn off some lights. I later took issue with him over this, pointing out that his action was paramount to a signal in British public houses that customers must leave forthwith as it was 'after hours', and that for world representatives this was inappropriate. However, the subsequent French hospitality for the teams, officials and delegates was excellent and all was soon forgiven.

Next day, the Pierre de Coubertin Stadium was the scene of day-long intense team contest activity, with three competition areas, one area only being used for the finals.

It is now well known that at these championships Great Britain was the first country to beat Japan. In the Bryn Williams book *Know Karate-do*, published in 1975, there is a concise account of the action in this important team contest against Japan, and this is reproduced with Bryn's permission, for which I am most grateful.

'In the first bout Stan Knighton fought Oishi, who for three years had been National Shotokan Champion of Japan. Everyone waited to see how long Knighton would last – but instead he attacked, taking the fight to Oishi and scoring a half point with *gyaku-zuki*, thus winning by judges' decision. This was a tremendous psychological boost to the British and a severe blow to the Japanese who had seen their champion defeated. In the next bout the British captain, Terry O'Neill, met Abe. For the entire bout Abe was forced to defend himself against a continuous barrage of roundhouse, back and side kicks and was unable to launch any decisive attack. Two of the four judges gave the decision to

O'Neill and the other two awarded a draw. When the referee awarded a draw the entire arena erupted in protest as O'Neill had clearly dominated the fight. Britain was unlucky not to be two matches ahead.

In the third fight Glen Haslam, although he put in some good attacks, was defeated by Iida, the first all-style Japanese champion. The team score was now equal. The fourth fight saw 5 ft 8 in. Hamish Adam against the 6 ft 2 in. Tabata who, although he had never won a major Japanese championship, had been runner up over a number of years. After a few near misses by Adam, Tabata decided the match was not going to be easy as his early contemptuous manner had implied. He mounted a sustained and fierce assault which Adam withstood. After continual contact Tabata was finally disqualified and Britain again led by 2 wins to 1 defeat with one draw.

Billy Higgins went into the final bout having only to draw for Britain to go through to the quarter finals. The atmosphere in the stadium was very hushed and tense as everyone realised they might be seeing history in the making. Higgins went out against Tanaka determined to win rather then draw. Tanaka, however, was equally determined and the result was a draw. Britain had defeated Japan.

The Japanese officials sportingly congratulated the British Team. For us, it was as though suddenly discovering that night did not follow day, that grass was not green, so great was this victory. Bryn Williams continued, 'For the next ten minutes the Coubertin stadium was a total shambles. Reporters ran out of the building as if Samson had caused the roof to collapse.'

France went on to beat Great Britain 3–nil with two draws and moved on to the final against Italy, which France won 3–1 with one draw, to become the 1972 World Champions.

The next day Higgins, in the individual championship, reached the final, where he was beaten by Watanabe from Brazil. Donovan and Wade, Great Britain, reached the last eight. Overall it was a very satisfactory performance by the whole British group. There was much celebration, and I was glad that we had the exclusive use of the hotel so that other guests would not be disturbed by the impromptu British party.

The 3rd World Karate Championships, Long Beach, USA, 1975

Encouraged by successes in the 1972 Paris Championships, and the experience thus gained, we had good time to prepare for Long Beach in 1975. Selections and training for the Great Britain team under the control of Steve Arneil took place at LJS in South London, Stratford in East London and in Manchester. I attended all these sessions as an observer. The Great Britain team was going to California with high hopes and a very good chance of total success, having been first to beat the Japanese national team in 1972 and subsequently to beat France, World Champions, at Crystal Palace in 1973 at the Fanfare for Europe match.

First there were political problems to sort out, such as which United States sports organisation would host the 3rd World Championships. I was telephoned from Japan, asking if I would go to Portland, Oregon to attend the 1st World Union of Karate-do Organisations (WUKO) Directing Committee meeting due on 15 and 16 May, 1974. I took leave from Wood Street, flying by Pan Am, at the expense of the Federation of All Japan Karate-do Organisations (FAJKO). At the Portland hotel I shared a room with Terry Wingrove, who fourteen years previously trained in Judo at Snow Hill police station, London, and was now advising FAJKO and WUKO in Japan.

A problem was that the 1st Vice President of WUKO, A R Allen (USA), wished to host the championships in the name of the All America Karate Federation (AAKF), a Japan Karate Association (Shotokan) group, whereas WUKO correctly insisted that the championships must be hosted by the body officially recognised by the Amateur Athletic Union of the United States (AAU), the principal USA sports authority. The president of the AAU, D R Rivenes, attended with J D Stevens, National Sports Administrator. These two men were the senior figures of USA national athletics.

It was a shame that the Japan Karate Association – with an efficient worldwide organisation specialising in shotokan style – tried to obtain the organisation of the 3rd World Championships. This was clearly the prerogative of WUKO, Japan based, with seventy-two countries in membership, and it did no credit to the JKA to attempt to alter this by political manoeuvre. It was activity like this that made Jacques Delcourt so sensitive. The BKCC had signed the WUKO statutes in Japan in 1970, with other nations present, thus becoming one of the founder members, so the JKA was ill-advised to challenge authority in this way.

Meetings in the Portland hotel continued late into the night and I was able to negotiate and reason in an independent capacity, though firmly in support of the WUKO position. I subsequently received a letter of thanks from FAJKO for my role in the corridor negotiations which helped to bring about a correct solution and unity. The JKA withdrew.

The downtown Portland hotel dining room ceiling was as familiar as it was memorable, being a large scale map of the City of London, where I had years ago 'pulled a lot of padlocks'. The waitresses were in delightful miniskirted 'Tower of London Beefeater' uniform with hats. However, I could not agree with the statement in the menu that the restaurant was based on the design of premises which used to stand at the junction of Bevis Marks and Lime Street – an impossibility; I think they meant Bevis Marks/St Mary Axe. The food was superb, and on the final night the French and American delegates had a discussion on the merits of French and Californian wines, buying the best on the wine list to make their point. I was pleased that I had no responsibility for the bill, but the wine was beautiful. I first considered every sip in terms of how much it was costing, then decided not to bother and just enjoy it like the rest of the party.

The 3rd World Championships were due on 4 and 5 October, 1975 in the Long Beach Arena. Bryn Williams was now working full-time as General Secretary of the BKCC, which was of immense benefit. A WUKO directive from Japan arrived, stating that a passport check would be made of all competitors and officials to ensure they had the nationality of the country they were representing, and Bryn wrote to all team members to check.

Eugene Codrington, a hospital electrician from Birmingham, a key athlete in the team, responded that he still carried a St Lucia passport, even though he had lived in England with his family for eighteen years, having arrived with his parents when aged eighteen months! This was difficult. Arrangements were made with the Home Office, the Passport Office and the American Embassy that Eugene, with supporting letters from BKCC, could be processed in good time. I arranged for an off-duty City Police detective, who lived in single men's quarters above Wood Street police station, to meet Eugene at Euston Station, take him to the Home Office for 'processing', following that to the Passport Office in Petty France and finally to the American Embassy in Grosvenor Square, London. Eugene was granted citizenship, a passport and a visa for the USA in an amazingly short time. Two bunches of flowers and letters of appreciation were duly sent. It had been close... He was to play a key role in the forthcoming World Championships.

The headquarters, conference centre and main accommodation for the 3rd World Championships was to be the magnificent ex-RMS *Queen Mary*, now tied up in Long Beach as a hotel and tourist attraction. Brian Hammond, our treasurer, had played a key part in the Great Britain team arrangements. First he booked flights in good time to allow the team to be time-adjusted by the date of the contests. Next he arranged accommodation at the Edgewater Hyatt Hotel several miles away, where there was peace and quiet, a swimming pool and access to the beaches for training. This was a major factor, as it would remove us from the distracting hustle, bustle and pressure which would be the ongoing scene in the *Queen Mary*.

At the Edgewater Hyatt, Steve Arneil and his team trained early every morning, running along the golden sands of the Pacific beach and enjoying the sun. Several mornings I joined them, just to watch, and noted that they were very fit, time-adjusted and relaxed. Brian Hammond's role in getting the team to the USA early was proving to be a great help. Bryn and I noted that the much-fancied French team, staying in the *Queen Mary*, came out to America only a few days before the event with the intention of staying on for a holiday – a big mistake if one wishes to win at world level.

Politics Again

There was another political problem. The Japan Karate Association had staged a 'World Karate Championship' in Los Angeles a month before the official World Championships – presumably to upstage the AAU and WUKO. It was declared by the host organisers that anyone who had taken part in this JKA World championship would be barred from taking part in the official WUKO 3rd World Championship. Bryn and I were mandated by the BKCC that if the two British karateka who had openly and in good faith taken part in the JKA event were so banned, then we should withdraw the whole British team from the WUKO championship. Of the two members of the Shotokan British team, one was Terry O'Neill, an outstanding karateka who had attended the JKA Los Angeles event solely as a contestant in the shotokan-style competition. I did not agree with the BKCC decision, which I thought was extreme, but gambled that our logical open stance was negotiable and would be successful.

Bryn and I left the Edgewater Hyatt Hotel and moved into the *Queen Mary* so that we would now be on site at all hours for vital negotiations. In the end the Americans, led by Caylor Adkins, National Chairman of the AAU Karate Committee, conceded we had a point, that we had acted openly in allowing our shotokan members to compete in the JKA event if they wished. If all this sounds pettily complicated, it was. Our strength was that we, the BKCC, were an all-styles open organisation, embracing the whole of British karate. Some other countries did not have this advantage, as they were single-style orientated. Our gamble was successful: to have withdrawn the team would have been crazy and could have brought about my resignation (shades of Kipling's 'If').

Visitor to Wood Street

In September 1975, the Mayor of Santa Monica, California, visited London as an official guest of the Foreign Office. Other than knowing that Santa Monica was on the Pacific coast, I had neglected to do homework by looking up the precise location. The Mayor, an ex-police officer, was a genial, good-looking fellow, reminding me of the singer Nat King Cole. We showed him round the police station; then he took lunch with the senior officers, visited the museum, stables, transport, communications and administrative departments. As we took afternoon tea, prior to his departure, he asked if I was considering a visit to America. I told him that I was actually going to Long Beach the following week and staying at the Edgewater Hyatt Hotel. He said he would be in touch, though frankly I forgot about it. On arrival at the hotel I found the Mayor was as good as his word. In my room was a message from the Mayoral Office of Santa Monica, asking me to ring. I did so and was invited to dinner, but before that there was to be a daytime visit to the Los Angeles Police Department (LAPD) training centre.

I attended with Bryn Williams and Terry O'Neill of the British Team and editor of *Fighting Arts* magazine. We were greeted by the Mayor and Captain Munger, in charge of the LAPD Training Centre, who provided a memorable day. I was particularly interested in the computerised firearms training system, where one stands on 'the spot', gun ready, with lights out. A life-size moving dark picture unfolds, causing the pupil to make decisions. If the pupil fires, the scene is frozen, the lights go on, the bullet hole is highlighted and a discussion ensues. I found I had shot at my reflection in a mirror! This was first-class training. In the large restaurant there was a huge sign reading 'The more you sweat here the less you will bleed on the streets.' This day was the Mayor's 'thank you' for the hospitality in Wood Street, London. We were very appreciative. In the evening Peter Jordan, team medical officer, joined us for dinner, and the Chief of Police of Santa Monica attended. Next day it was back to business and the objective of winning the World Karate Championship.

Students at the LAPD Training Centre were introduced to us, and three were coming to London. I invited them to Wood Street and they duly came. To my surprise they were particularly interested in the police stables and riding kit, making notes as to where they could buy riding boots whilst in London. In the evening they came home for a meal, and the train journey to Petts Wood was memorable, for by sheer coincidence we met Leslie Morrison on London Bridge station. (See 'Cannon Row Stories'.

He showed me round beats twenty-five years previously and was an expert on the history of the Houses of Parliament.) One of the LAPD students was studying for a doctorate in London history, and their conversation during the next half-hour was intense and extraordinary. I hope she did well in her final presentation.

The RMS *Queen Mary*

It was with a feeling of national pride that at last I could walk on the decks and in the staterooms of *Queen Mary*. I had listened to the Clyde 1936 Royal Commissioning on radio (King Edward VIII and Queen Mary), cut out pictures, painted and sketched the ship and seen it with awe off the Isle of Wight. Painted grey, it had given excellent service as a troopship in the 1939–1945 war and was still doing duty in retirement. I was intrigued to find that all the ship's mirrors were of tinted peach-coloured glass, so that passengers on the Atlantic crossing would look at themselves and think they looked well – a nice touch.

I was relaxing with Bryn in our shared *Queen Mary* room when there was an unexpected knock at the door. 'President Sasakawa requests that you attend the WUKO Committee meeting immediately,' said the messenger. (I was not a member of the committee.) I hurriedly changed from casual to more formal dress and, adjusting my shirt and tie as I hurried along the corridors, duly presented myself at the committee room door. I politely bowed to the President and took the seat indicated at the WUKO Committee table. There were bright lights, and I was filmed on arrival. It was not until I sat down at the table that I thought about whether or not my shirt was properly tucked in and I furtively checked my zip too. I looked round the table, relieved that I had arrived properly dressed, but made a mental note never to rush like that again. 'The camera doesn't lie, m'lud…'

The Congress

Next event in the *Queen Mary* was the 3rd World Congress. Bryn and I were again the appointed delegates for Great Britain. I asked to address the Congress, at which all competing countries were represented, on the subject of the General Assembly of International Federations (GAIF). Briefed by Bryn, who had a major grasp of the politics, the Karate Congress was informed that the Japan Karate Association (JKA) had applied to join GAIF as the official international karate body, and had canvassed British delegates accordingly. The GAIF meeting was in Canada while we were at Long Beach. We had already written to the three British delegates to alert them and spoken to Charles Palmer, Chairman of the British Judo Association, and subsequently Chairman of the British Olympic Association. The Congress unanimously agreed that Charles Palmer should represent WUKO at the GAIF meeting and this was confirmed to him by cable. The result was that another political manoeuvre by the JKA was thwarted and the multilingual Charles Palmer became the General Secretary of GAIF.

With political problems solved for the time being, we now concentrated on the task of winning the championships. The daily training, led by Steve Arneil, was excellent and I continued to watch when possible, taking care not to join in. All were in very good shape and relaxed in the sun. A personnel carrier was available to convey the team to the Long Beach Arena and to the *Queen Mary*, where there was a reception for competitors and delegates. Back at our Edgewater Hyatt Hotel, we also had on-the-spot relaxation and entertainment, for as hotel residents we had free entry to a special onsite disco promotion – the Miss California Wet T-shirt Competition – with the famous football team, the Los Angeles Rams, as the judges. The competition was hilariously good fun and I envied the relaxed ability of the participants and judges to enjoy themselves. I relate this story because it was just another event helping our team to enjoy light relief, thus taking their minds momentarily off the huge imminent task ahead in the Long Beach Arena.

Shot and Sail

A memorable interlude occurred during our fourteen days at Long Beach. I hired a car and drove Peter and Bryn to Los Angeles, where we joined many Americans to board a reproduction sailing ship, complete with replica guns, cannonballs and reasonable catering facilities. The size of the container ships using this Pacific port is enormous, and great excitement ensued when our crew fired at one of these huge ships, using loud blanks with accompanying smoke: the container-ship crew must have thought we were mad! It was a good, fun example of the feel of 'shot and sail' in the 1800s. After leaving the ship in darkness and before driving back to Los Angeles, we tried to negotiate our way out of the harbour area. I came across some unusual traffic lights which we suddenly realised were railway lights. I hurriedly U-turned off the railway, exited the dock area and got away with it.

Saturday, 4 October arrived. Our team was carefully looked after by Steve Arneil, who showed great leadership skills. His team briefings, which I attended but did not participate in, save to wish the competitors well, were exceptional, and he had brought them to a peak at the correct time. The official programme published forewords from Gerald R Ford, President of the United States, Member of Congress Mark Hannaford, and Dr Thomas Clark, Mayor of Long Beach. The Arena was huge and the competition was to commence at 10 a.m.

Belgium had beaten the USA in the first round and was paired with Great Britain in the second round. This match we won comfortably, and so on to the third round where we met South Africa, who had previously eliminated Mexico and Canada. The coach of the South Africa team was Norman Robinson, a brother of the famous Robinson judo brothers, Joe and Doug. Norman Robinson was instructing his team using the Afrikaans language. Fortunately for us, Steve Arneil understood what Norman was briefing and gave our team counter-instructions; another string to Steve's bow. South Africa was duly beaten, and now we moved into the semi-finals to meet the Philippines, who had previously defeated Guatemala, China and Germany. Our defeat of the Philippines took us into the final against Japan. Our eagerly awaited contest for the World Championship was against a Japan team, which on the way had defeated the Netherlands, Singapore, Switzerland and New Zealand.

Meanwhile, in close liaison with other members of the British party, Steve Arneil had carefully watched our competitors and was able to give the team last-minute advice.

One magazine said this:

Steve Arneil was the soul of the team, encouraging without being ruffled, keeping his sense of humour and entertaining the audience with a dialogue with one of the South African fans.

The French called him 'The Fox', a compliment.

Now to the climax of the whole event: the final. There was much anticipation and tension. Billy Higgins, team captain, won his contest against Takizawa, Brian Fitkin lost by two *waza-ari*, Eugene Codrington kept attacking Yonemitsu with kicking techniques and was unlucky not to score or be awarded the contest. Newly selected Gene Dunnett scored twice against his opponent to win his contest, and now the crowd could detect another sensation – it all depended on the last contest with Hamish Adam against Murakami. Hamish had either to win or draw. Hamish showed some brilliant kicking techniques and was unlucky not to score – one observer thought a Hamish attempt was so fast that the referee and judges did not see it! The result was a draw, making the Great Britain team World Champions, a planned and calculated triumph for Steve Arneil and the team. The crowd gave a rousing standing ovation, and Ryoichi Sasakawa, President of WUKO, presented the huge World Championship trophy to captain Billy Higgins.

The Japanese were very sporting in defeat. Ryoichi Sasakawa, President, dismounted from the stage and, with his entourage, sought me out in the audience to congratulate on behalf of the whole Great Britain contingent. I duly conveyed this to all. I could hardly believe it – all the planning, training and cooperation had come to fruition. The ideal dream came true on this day.

After the event we went back to the hotel, but celebrations had to be reasonably subdued as some members of the team were due back at the Long Beach Arena next day for the individual competition; our main celebrations could come later. Back at the Edgewater Hyatt Hotel, the staff there had reacted quickly, for a huge illuminated sign shone out across the massive boating marina and to sea, spelling out our success: 'Congratulations Great Britain – World Karate Champions'. The Americans are good at this sort of thing. That was the start, and a lot more was to follow.

Our referees, Brian Hammond, Thomas Morris, Roy Stanhope and John Lowcock, had worked well. Earlier I referred to the fact that the French team and officials had made a mistake in arriving just a few days before the championships, for they would not be time-adjusted or acclimatised to Long Beach. I believe this affected their star performer, Dominique Valera, several times European Champion and exceptional karateka, who was disqualified and banned. He had tried to roundhouse-kick Tommy Morris (*jodan mawashi geri*), tried to punch Roy Stanhope, and then performed a flying kick (*yoko tobi geri*) on seated judge Peter Rousseau (South Africa), knocking him over – all were acting in their official capacities at the time. I saw it happening and could hardly believe it. Brian Hammond was refereeing another match on an adjacent raised area and had an excellent view of the incident. Brian felt that Valera must have controlled his attacks, which would otherwise have caused serious injury if delivered with full power.

This incident was reported in headlines 'Valera Flips' and 'Valera triggers karate riot'. Police were called and he was later banned for life, leaving the championships forthwith. I believe his late arrival at the championships, possible lack of sleep and time adjustment were contributory causes for this brilliant karateka to break under stress. Once again I considered how lucky we were to have arrived early, but it meant leaving Los Angeles the day after the championships – job done. In the hotel I received several calls from British radio stations very early next morning, the day after the championship, and the interviews were syndicated to several million listeners and viewers during Sunday in Great Britain.

Congratulatory telegrams began to arrive, which I read out in the coach on the way to Los Angeles Airport. We heard from Denis Howell, the Minister for Sport, the Chairman of the Sports Council, Dr Sir Roger Bannister, and one from Denis Delderfield, member of the Police Committee and Common Council for the City of London, which I shall enlarge upon later.

On the Trans World Airways Boeing 747 return flight, the pilot made an announcement welcoming the team and their karate success and the World Trophy was taken through the plane by members and displayed to the passengers. It was a very happy flight. I did not sleep on the journey home.

At Heathrow at 6.30 a.m. the press photographers were already there, and pictures and press interviews appeared in the course of the next few days. Cartoonists had some fun, too.

Steve Arneil took several team members to Pebble Mill, Birmingham, to demonstrate and be interviewed on live television. Michael Parkinson was on the same show. I asked him to sign the signatory page of the officials and competitors from Long Beach, and this page is reproduced in this book. Ticky Donovan took some young karateka to Thames Television studios to appear in the children's television *Magpie* programme.

Back in London, Denis Delderfield was soon to play a very helpful part. First he contacted the marshal responsible for assembly of the Lord Mayor's Show (this procession always takes place annually on the second Saturday in November) to ascertain if there was still a float vacancy. There was. Next he contacted Whitbread (John Fox, the public relations officer), who confirmed availability of a brand-new Whitbread's lorry. (Whitbread's lorries were always in first-class condition.) We had a meeting at Whitbread's, and Denis followed that with a contact to paint and decorate the lorry with a karate theme up to Lord Mayor's Show standard. The link was to be the World Karate Trophy and Whitbread's Trophy Bitter – a good combination. Bryn circulated the team and referees, and Mary Williams circulated parents of young children at her school, asking them to allow their youngsters to appear in the Lord Mayor's Show around the float, with 'Karate is great' banners. Bryn organised twenty junior karate suits, and luckily the weather was kind on the day. All in all, it was an excellent, topical entry, which was very well received.

On the day of the procession I was as usual on duty in uniform at the Bank junction opposite the Mansion House and felt very proud and pleased for the team members, young supporters and the karate float as the World Trophy passed by, to be acknowledged by the Lord Mayor of London on the balcony. It was yet another a moment I shall not forget. Whitbread's had been very helpful to us.

The *Daily Express*

It did not end there. As the float progressed along Fleet Street it came under scrutiny from the national press and was seen by

Sir Max Aitken of the *Daily Express* (himself a Battle of Britain pilot). Next, the team was invited to the Savoy Hotel for the *Daily Express* Sport of the Year Awards to be broadcast by *World of Sport*, London Weekend Television. Dickie Davies was the compère, and Tony McCarthy (of the BKFC) was in the production team. To my complete surprise, our victorious World Championship Karate Team was presented with the Sports Team of the Year Award. The team, in 'uniform' of Great Britain blazers, was well turned out, and the award well received. We had been on national television. The *Daily Express* ran subsequent backup articles on the team; one story with pictures, unfortunate for the England football team, compared scruffily dressed footballers with the immaculate turnout of the award-winning karate team.

Previous winners of the *Daily Express* Sports Team of the Year Trophy were:

1971   Elf Team Tyrrell – Ken Tyrrell

1972   Three-Day Event Gold Medal British Olympic Equestrian Team. Richard Mead, Bridget Parker, Mary Gordon-Watson, Mark Phillips

1973   Sunderland Football Club, Football Association Cup Winners

1974   British Lions Rugby Team

1975   British Karate Team, World Champions

I eventually kept that trophy safely at Wood Street police station, as it had to be returned after one year and we had 'lost' some other notable trophies, I suspect to clubs in the North, where they were highly valued, having been exhibited at numerous events.

We were also advised that we were front runners for the end-of-year BBC Sports Team of the Year award, but alas, though we tried, no film footage could be retrieved from Long Beach, and one cannot possibly be considered for that very public award if there is no available film coverage! However, members of the team were invited to the BBC ceremony, receiving a 'mention', and this was, in the circumstances, more recognition indeed.

Medical Backup

As the BKCC progressed and member associations conducted their own championships, it was agreed there should be adequate first aid and medical assistance at all competitions. This became the standard, and member associations developed their own contacts with the St John Ambulance Association and local doctors. Young doctors in particular were well motivated and keen on sport, and it was usual, towards the end of an event, to announce how much their presence had been appreciated. They were always well applauded.

An occasion when medical advice and help was needed was soon after the selection of the Great Britain Team for the first 1970 World Championships in Japan. There had been a serious outbreak of a tropical disease in the Far East and it was a requirement for all eastbound travellers to receive vaccination before departure. Certification of vaccination had first to be presented in the country of boarding.

There followed a big demand and consequent shortage of available vaccine in some areas. It would have been risky to rely on team members to organise their own protection locally. Time was important. I remembered my national service days when we queued for vaccinations and the subsequent swollen and tender arms – not good for karate competition – so the sooner the team could recover from the effects of the protection the better it would be.

I went to see my neighbour, Dr Roger May, ex-Guy's Hospital First Fifteen Rugby, a general practitioner highly regarded in Chislehurst, where he had a surgery. He undertook the task willingly, attending a dojo at Stratford, East London, on a Sunday where Steve Arneil, British Team Manager, was conducting a training session. All were vaccinated in ample time for recovery and we were very grateful.

Later in the year, the first BKCC All Styles championship was

This photograph, taken in the early 1900s near Guildhall, City of London, shows the original use of armlets as worn in the days when police wore top hats and morning dress: sergeants on the right arm, constables on the left arm (inspectors' armlets were worn halfway up the left arm). Alan Francis's grandfather is on the left.

Photograph courtesy of the City of London Police Museum.

Alan Francis sits next to Betty White in the front row at Lawn Lane School, South Lambeth Road near Brixton, London 1937.

*The ruins of 66 Beverley Gardens, Wembley, after it was bombed on 29 September 1940.
Six people were killed next door at Number 64.*

Photograph by David Buckley.

The family later moved to the house on the other side of the road, visible in the background of this photograph. All film went to the war effort, so a private picture like this is rare.

Photograph by David Buckley.

Alan Francis aged nineteen with the 'Station Dog'
during his National Service at RAF Station Cosford, 1949.

Alan at the Norwegian tree in Trafalgar Square during his first Christmas with the Metropolitan Police, 1950. Later that night the Coronation Stone was taken from Westminster Abbey by Scottish Nationalists.

The Metropolitan Police Wrestling and Judo Section on the occasion of the retirement of the Chairman Deputy Commander, H P Ralph OBE MC, 22 October 1955. Alan Francis is rear row, third from left, while George Chew is front row, far right. Inspector Stan Bissell (front row, fifth from right) was an Olympic wrestler and judo black belt.

The City Police on show in the Barbican, 1969. Front row (left to right): Commander A MacGregor, Commissioner James Page, Chairman Bernard Morgan and Assistant Commissioner Walter Stapleton.

Photograph by Robert Hope, the Daily Telegraph.

General Secretary of the British Karate Control Commission
Bryn Williams, BSc (Econ), DLC.

The first team to beat Japan. Steve Arneil, Team Manager, with the Great Britain team at Crystal Palace, April 1972. Billy Higgins (front row left) was a finalist.

Photograph by Robert Hope.

Meeting the Japanese delegation at the New Tokyo Restaurant, Swallow Street, London, 1972. Left to Right: Tatsuo Suzuki, Tom Hibbert, Eiichi Eriguchi, Alan Francis, Ryoichi Sasakawa (President, WUKO), Hideo Tsuchiya (Head Liaison Officer, WUKO), Bryn Williams, Hauyoshi Kagawa (Congress Delegate, Japan), Mitsusuke Harada and Keinosuke Enoeda.

Dr Roger Bannister, Chairman of the Sports Council, came to the Martini Terrace, New Zealand House to meet the Great Britain team and wish them well for the Paris Championship. Billy Higgins (left) was runner-up in the final of the individual competition at the World Championship, 1972.

Photograph by Robert Hope.

The City of London Police deal with large volumes of commuters in a bustling city. Alan Francis arranged this photograph of a morning scene at London Bridge, 1973. Photograph by Robert Hope, the Daily Telegraph.

The proprietor of a Valencia night club (standing, left) with members of the Valencia Police and guests during the European Championships, 1973. Seated at the table (left to right): Alan Francis (BKCC), Peter Jordan (Medical Officer, BKCC) and Prince Adan Czyartoriski-Bourbon of Spain.

The Presentation of the Order of Civil Merit to Rhee Ki Ha, Chief Instructor to the United Kingdom Tae Kwon Do Association at Claridges Hotel. Left to right: Mr and Mrs Choi, His Excellency the Ambassador for Korea, Rhee Ki Ha and Alan Francis.

Photograph courtesy of UKTA.

The first WUKO Directing Comittee during the preparations for the 1975 3rd World Championships, May 1974. Left to right: James Stevens (National Sport Administrator, The Amateur Athletic Union of the USA), Alan Francis (Chairman, BKCC), Eiichi Eriguchi (Secretary, WUKO) and Jacques Delcourt (Chairman, WUKO).

Ticky Donovan and Billy Higgins (holding the World Karate Trophy) on the Lord Mayor's Show float in Cheapside, London, November 1975.

Photograph by Brian Hammond.

The Daily Express *Sports Team of the Year Trophy, which the British Karate Team Champions won in 1975. It was presented at the Savoy Hotel.*

Photograph by John Lancaster, City of London Police.

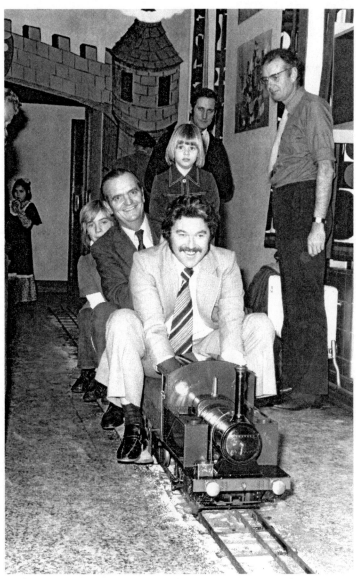

Dicky Davies, presenter of World of Sport *(London Weekend TV), drives the train at the Wood Street Police Station Charity Children's Christmas Party.*
Photograph Courtesy of the City of London Police.

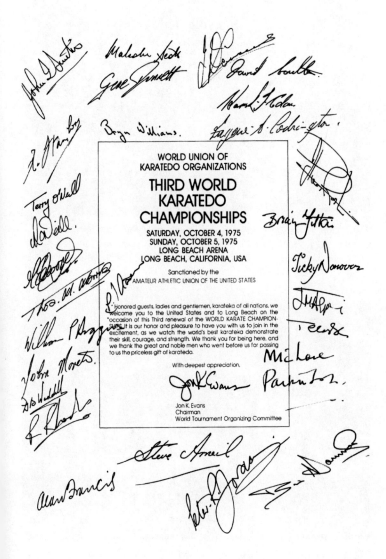

WORLD UNION OF
KARATEDO ORGANIZATIONS

THIRD WORLD KARATEDO CHAMPIONSHIPS

SATURDAY, OCTOBER 4, 1975
SUNDAY, OCTOBER 5, 1975
LONG BEACH ARENA
LONG BEACH, CALIFORNIA, USA

Sanctioned by the
AMATEUR ATHLETIC UNION OF THE UNITED STATES

Honored guests, ladies and gentlemen, karateka of all nations, we welcome you to the United States and to Long Beach on the occasion of this Third renewal of the WORLD KARATE CHAMPIONSHIPS. It is our honor and pleasure to have you with us to join in the excitement, as we watch the world's best karateka demonstrate their skill, courage, and strength. We thank you for being here, and we thank the great and noble men who went before us for passing to us the priceless gift of karatedo.

With deepest appreciation,

Jon K. Evans
Chairman
World Tournament Organizing Committee

This page in the programme for the 3rd World Championships includes the original signatures for the whole team. When they appeared on the same TV show as Michael Parkinson, he also signed it.

The referees for the 3rd World Championships. Back Row (left to right) – Great Britain: Brian Hammond, John Lowcock, Roy Stanhope and Tommy Morris. Front Row (left to right) – Japan: Hiroshi Kinjo, Teruo Hayashi, Kenei Maburi and Manzo Iwata (all 10th Dan).

Photograph by Brian Hammond.

The formation of the Martial Arts Comission. Sir Derek Capper (Chairman) welcomes the new General Secretary, David Mitchell PhD (left) and says goodbye to the retiring General Secretary, Bryn Williams (right).

Photograph courtesy of Combat *Magazine*

Here the late Keinosuke Enoeda demonstrates to a KUGB course at the National Sports Centre, Crystal Palace. This photograph was used in the brochure 'Karate… the mis-understood [sic] sport'.

Photograph by Robert Hope (for BKCC).

New Cross Riots, 1977: Trouble about to start. Note the different helmet design.
Photograph courtesy of PA Photos.

Tony Leung with Chuck Norris on the set of one of his kung fu films in Hong Kong
Photograph courtesy of Tony Leung.

Tony Leung (centre) with members of his London kung fu club.

The Boxing Day kung fu demonstration at the Old Corner House, Coventry Street. Previously operated by J Lyons and Co, the building was now a Chinese Restaurant.

Billy Higgins, Ticky Donovan and Eugene Codrington of the successful British team and Brian Hammond (right), referee, with two young assistants on the Lord Mayor's Show float in 1975 (about to pass Wood Street Police Station).

Photograph courtesy of Brian Hammond.

The Lord Mayor of London, Sir Robin Gillett, recieves a certificate of Honorary Dan from Ryochi Sasakawa, President of WUKO, during his visit to Mansion House.
Photographs courtesy of the City of London Corporation.

held at Crystal Palace National Sports Centre. All the member associations cooperated, and it was one huge undertaking with three competition areas intensively in use throughout the day. Crystal Palace was packed, and catering and general staff were kept very busy. Dr Roger May attended as medical officer and once again gave valuable service. He later reported that at one time he had in his medical room no less than six karateka in various stages of unconsciousness, plus all the other more minor incidents needing his attention. (Referees' and judges' courses were placed high on the agenda as a result of this, and there was much general improvement as experience developed, bringing about better competitor protection.)

So we began the search for a new medical officer, and I asked sports colleagues in the City Police if they knew of a suitable person. The name Peter R Jordan came forward from John Cardwell, a prominent member of the police swimming team. Peter Jordan, a plastic surgeon, trained in St Bartholomew's Hospital, City of London. He had also qualified as a physical education teacher at Loughborough College, then financed his subsequent medical training by professional wrestling, an astonishing combination: just the man for the BKCC. He readily agreed to help and the first undertaking, with many to follow, was at the 1972 2nd World Karate Championship in Paris.

I was concerned how such a respected medical practitioner would settle with the team. He was to share a room in Paris with Brian Crowley, British referee, ex-Metropolitan Police. I need not have worried as they got on so well – both spoke fluent French, and this was very useful. Peter Jordan also spoke Spanish. The World Championship organisers were so impressed that he was promptly appointed medical officer for the 1972 World Championships – who better? Indirectly, this enhanced the status of the British delegation, as word went round the delegates that the British doctor was multilingual and highly qualified. Peter Jordan's support to the team members in the hotel was also valuable, the ready availability of good advice on diet, knocks, aches and pains giving much peace of mind.

At the next European Championships in Valencia, Spain, Peter's presence was a blessing to team member, Brian Fitkin. In the Sunday competition, Brian suffered severe injury to his jaw when he was accidentally struck by a foot technique which pushed in his top front teeth. The liaison officer for the British team was a Spanish policemen, who got them to the local hospital, only to find the accident department was closed. Mary Williams with Peter Jordan, using Spanish, got the staff to open the operating theatre. Using fuse wire, he reshaped and repaired Brian's jaw and teeth, restoring them to their original position. 'That will do us until we get back home on Monday,' said Peter. This backup also gave a huge boost of confidence to all the remaining team members, just from knowing this knowledge and skill was behind them in the event of need.

Word reached the local police that I was a London policeman and an invitation (the sort one cannot refuse) arrived at the hotel to say that at 10.30 p.m. transport would collect me and a guest to attend the Valencia Police Headquarters. Properly dressed in our England uniform of blazers, flannels and ties, and having enjoyed a bottle of wine in the hotel, Peter and I went to inspect the night-duty police who were paraded and at attention. We duly slowly walked the ranks and I suitably thanked them. They looked formidable, dressed in black leather, and in a roughhouse I would be pleased to know I was on their side. It did not end there. After a tour of the headquarters we were taken to a nightclub in town to watch the cabaret. Also present was Prince Adan Czartoryski-Bourbon of Spain, a karate supporter and brilliant trilingual verbatim interpreter at the European Union Karate Congress. (There are some very able people about.) The police, in uniform, also came into the club and watched, but no one seemed to bother about this. It occurred to me that this would not (or should not) happen in the cities of London or Westminster! It was a very late night, and we had a lot to do next day. I recall the police courtesy and hospitality with affection.

When Belgium hosted the European Championships in Ostend, Brian Hammond organised the direct flight. We flew direct from Southend Airport in an old-style passenger/freight plane, which in itself was an experience. Peter Jordan again helped and his ongoing humour contributed to a very happy party with excellent team spirit. Brian Hammond was given the honour of officiating in the final of the European Championships, and did so with distinction.

Peter Jordan flew with the British Team to Long Beach, California, for the early October 1975 World Championships. (In European competition, England, Scotland and Wales formed separate teams, but in world competition we combined to form a British Team.) Thirty-eight countries competed, and once again Peter was welcomed as the medical officer. This event is described in the chapter covering the 1975 3rd World Championships.

Back in Great Britain, one of the most successful policy outcomes was that of medical/first-aid provision at competitions. It was certainly appreciated and of benefit to the competitors. Weekend residential courses for referees and judges were held by BKCC, and the European Karate Union, usually at Easter, ran courses for those wishing to qualify at international level. All this activity combined to reduce accidents and give competitors confidence and knowledge that their interests were in good hands.

Cannon Row Stories

As a young probationer I was attached to a senior constable to learn beats and pick up the 'feel' of being in uniform. One of these senior constables was Leslie Morrison, a Scot, who came to London to join the Police in the 1930s via coal boat from the North East, a cheap method of travel, to berth in the Thames near Battersea Power Station. These coal boats were called 'flat irons' as they had a low superstructure to enable them to negotiate the low bridges. Leslie Morrison went on to become a leading guide and authority on the history of the Houses of Parliament. In January 1973 he showed the national karate team of France round the Houses of Parliament prior to the Fanfare for Europe match at Crystal Palace, described separately in the chapter 'The European Scene'. When arranging this visit I forgot the fact that there are two huge murals in the House, one of the Battle of Waterloo and the other the Battle of Trafalgar; these victories took place in the early 1800s – part of our rich historical involvement with France.

I now relate some early experiences in Trafalgar Square and Westminster, which helped shape my formative years in the police service, giving a perspective on 'fair play' and judgement, some of which I got right.

First Arrest

When eventually allowed out on my own I enjoyed direct contact with the public, and Trafalgar Square was a very busy posting to experience just that. It was not long before a smart, well-dressed young lady of about thirty years approached me, indicating her swollen lip and alleging that she had been assaulted by a costermonger in the Strand outside what was then Lyons Corner House. Still imbued with Peel House training, I went with her to the scene, asking that she repeat in front of the costermonger what she had just told me. She related that she wanted two pears only and had been charged too much, certainly more than the advertised price per pound: she wanted her money back. What happened next I could hardly believe, but I remember it in slow motion. His right arm swung widely and he hit her face hard with the back of his hand, known as a 'backhander'. That was it. In shock I momentarily forgot all about Peel House procedure. 'Right, you're nicked!' I said impulsively, taking him to the nearest police post. I had also to see to the victim, a vital witness, and think about the security of his barrow of fruit, an open target for free samples, whether in the street or the police yard!

Next day the costermonger appeared at Bow Street, pleading not guilty before magistrate Paul Bennett VC, MC. I gave evidence up to Peel House standard and, fingers crossed, told the magistrate that the accused was told he was being arrested. He was duly dealt with. Next day, JAJ, a columnist writing 'Courts Day by Day' in the London *Evening News*, humorously reported the event headed 'Two make a fine pear' – my first arrest was now an article in the London press.

I must add here that it was always a privilege to give evidence before Paul Bennett. He won the Victoria Cross in Le Transoy in the 1914–1918 war: though injured and armed only with a spade he led a successful charge at the enemy. When he retired in 1961, the West End costermongers, most of whom had appeared before him, made a collection and presented him with a magnificent leather hamper with hallmarked silver contents.

'The doctor said I was drunk...'

Late on a Saturday, a man hopelessly drunk was trying to cross the road at Trafalgar Square, a danger to himself and others. He just had to be arrested for his own protection. As I approached, he held on to a lamppost outside South Africa House and would not let go. Luckily a police van was passing and the crew helped me get him aboard. The lamppost remained upright. At Cannon Row police station, where he was barely able to stand, he insisted he was not drunk and demanded to see a doctor to prove his sobriety. The great shipping industry of this country was being reduced, making many seamen redundant; hitherto ships had been their homes, but they were now homeless. This fellow was one of those affected, all money spent on drink to 'drown the sorrow' and numb the brain. Doctors were always difficult to call out in the 1950s; they understandably did not wish to attend the station, running the risk of having to be at court, followed by missing a surgery. In any case, the ex-seaman had no money to pay for his requested doctor.

A sergeant, whom I remember well, put on a white traffic coat, pretended to be a doctor and, after making his patient undergo various tests, like walking a none-too-straight chalk line, declared the seaman drunk.

Next morning at Bow Street he pleaded guilty before magistrate Bertram Rees. 'Have you anything to say?' asked the magistrate. 'Yes,' said the accused, 'I didn't think I was drunk but the doctor said I was drunk, so I've pleaded guilty.'

Bertram Rees looked at the back of the charge sheet: no doctor signature. 'Doctor? Doctor? You didn't have a doctor; you *must* have been drunk. Any trouble, officer?' I confirmed no trouble. 'Fine forty shillings.'

'The accused has no means to pay, Your Worship,' volunteered the gaoler. The penalty was then altered to one day in prison, meaning the accused could leave after the court had risen (and without a heavy medical bill).

Short cuts like this were a simple cost-effective way of facilitating very fair justice, but it was risky. I had reservations and considered one strike was enough, but as the next story will reveal, there was another 'short cut' about to happen.

Peeping Tom

There was the sad case of a man who persisted in looking up the clothing of women and girls who were bending down to feed Trafalgar Square pigeons. These days he would have difficulty, for nearly all the ladies wear trousers or jeans. This particular man was so blatant and oblivious to others' reactions that I thought he would soon be assaulted. I stood in front of him to give him the message, but I might as well not have bothered: he was so intent upon his purpose that he had not even seen me. So I arrested him for insulting behaviour likely to cause a breach of the peace, and he came peacefully to Cannon Row. It transpired that he was an army captain in charge of transport at his military base. This complicated matters. We would now have to notify his commanding officer, and a representative of the army would also have to attend court. I felt the whole incident was getting out of proportion and began to wish I had taken another course of action. The problem with that was that if I had accused him verbally and taken no further action, I was exposed if he then complained and I had done nothing further at the scene. Experienced policemen advised that if any action is needed, firm action is better than weak action; I am now not so sure about that. It is all a question of balance.

At Cannon Row, the Captain was taken aside by the Station Officer. It was agreed that if his occupation was entered on the charge sheet as 'Transport Manager', then we need not notify his army base in the West Country and the matter would go through court with less risk of publicity. We were trying to be kind and he agreed. Next morning I attended Bow Street in uniform, where once again the respected Bertram Rees was the magistrate. The accused pleaded guilty but I was very concerned when he arrived at court immaculately dressed, carrying a lined bowler hat and displaying a very well-known regimental tie. I believe the magistrate quickly spotted this. He held in his hand the charge sheet, on which 'Transport Manager' was a slender truth. The accused had nothing to say except that he was sorry and the magistrate then said, ' I think I shall remand you in custody for a week for a medical report.' (My heart sank. This will expose our deception, I thought, and I shall be in deep trouble.) Mr Rees continued, 'But instead you will pay a fine of £5 and I wish never to see you in court again.'

What a relief! The shrewd magistrate got the penalty exactly right, and the army officer and I had learned a huge lesson. I told the Station Officer that this had been a 'near miss'.

A few years of these experiences was like going through a University of the Streets!

The Coronation Stone

At Christmas in 1950, in Trafalgar Square the tree from Norway (possibly the first year of the trees as a 'thank you' for war services) attracted large crowds including nurses from nearby Charing Cross Hospital, now Charing Cross police station. Carols were sung and everyone was happy. There followed an influx of youths with Mediterranean complexions, among others, who started to molest the nurses and other young ladies, and we stepped in to stop it. Fights and arrests followed until midnight and at one stage we were thankfully helped by a passing Royal Military Police mobile patrol. At 12.30 a.m., now Christmas Day, I was due to relieve Constable Phil Pedwell in the Westminster Abbey area, and telephoned the station to say that I was heavily engaged at Trafalgar Square. I was told to stay there. By 6 a.m. we were off duty. Phil Pedwell took me on his motorcycle to Victoria, where we all lived in the police hostel called Ambrosden Section House. I arranged with him that we would mutually ensure that we were awake by twelve noon in order to get to our respective homes, there being no public transport on Christmas Day.

When I arose at noon I went to Phil Pedwell's room – he was not there. I washed and shaved and went to the canteen before cycling to Wembley for lunch with the family. Phil Pedwell was in the canteen. I remonstrated with him for leaving me in my room, potentially asleep, when we had each agreed to ensure the other was awake. He looked tired and pale and said he had been up since ten o'clock, as there had been trouble at the Abbey. I was in a hurry and did not stop to question it.

I cycled hard to Wembley, arriving home just in time for the one o'clock radio news. First item: the Coronation Stone had been stolen from Westminster Abbey. I was uneasy, as I should have been there, but one cannot be in two places at once and I had been busy in Trafalgar Square. The Stone of Scone, which had been in the Abbey since 1297, had been removed by Scottish Nationalists. Years later I was to read an account of the venture written for the *Readers Digest* by one of the Scottish team, and in 2006 I read an obituary in the *Daily Telegraph* of another conspirator, who had become a Queen's Counsel in Scotland. I mused that if this had happened in the reign of Elizabeth I they would have been executed. The incident cost many thousands of hours of police time. The Serpentine, Welsh Harp reservoir and some areas of the River Thames were searched and hoaxers complicated the investigation.

May Day Demonstration

On 1 May in the early 1950s, in Trafalgar Square there was a May Day rally and demonstration led by left-wing activists and supporters. Police became aware that very soon there would be a march on Downing Street, and urgent precautions were taken as in those days Downing Street was open, like a normal street. Two police lorries were placed across Downing Street and foot police stood in front of the lorries, unsure what was going to happen next. Inspector 'Jock' Hutcheson, who was later the toast of Cannon Row canteen, took charge. He alerted his men that if he felt we were coming under pressure he would give the command 'Draw sticks', whereupon we were to stand with truncheons erect and wait for the demonstrators to make the next move. In the event, the demonstrators saw this disciplined 'drill' of truncheons and stopped, coming no further. Next, a delegation was allowed to deliver a letter to No. 10. I was impressed.

I always remembered the reaction of the demonstrators to this display of drill by foot police, and the scene now changes to Barbican, City of London in 1967, when major building contractors (Wates, Taylor Woodrow and Myton) were crippled by an eighteen-month-old strike organised by activists. There was a similar 'sister' strike at sites in Millbank, SW1. The contractors announced that all strikers were to be sacked and a new labour force signed on. When the strikers announced that they would prevent the new labour force reporting for work, trouble was anticipated. The City Police had an early 6 a.m. muster on this day; many officers slept in Bishopsgate and Wood Street stations in order to be on duty in time, and approximately 150 men were available. I was a Chief Inspector at this time, and my role was to attend the Wood Street muster for the initial disposition of police in Barbican. I drove to work at 5 a.m. for I could not risk being late in the event of train failure. En route to the City, and anticipating trouble ahead, I reminisced to myself about the Downing Street incident fifteen years previously, and considered briefing all concerned at Wood Street that if we were threatened with violent confrontation I would give the order 'Draw sticks!' and then see what resulted. There was an active 'buzz' getting a large number of police organised at that time of the morning, and some had made valiant efforts, walking, cycling et cetera, to ensure punctuality. In the confusion and pressure of time I absolutely forgot to mention truncheons. It was too late; I would just have to abandon the idea. To make a disciplined drill impression when all concerned were not expecting it was now out of the question. I was anxious about the possible outcome at the scene.

There was a confrontation with pushing and shoving, and punches were thrown, resulting in some injuries and arrests (many arrested had never worked on a building site) but no truncheons were drawn. The new workforce was signed on. The strike ended. The press were very impressed and some experienced newsmen wrote personally to Sir Arthur Young, City Police Commissioner, to congratulate the Force on the way it handled the situation. I just kept quiet, counting my blessings! The strike, outcome and the question of police restraint later featured in the BBC programme, *Panorama*.

An Embankment Gun

National service in the RAF Police had given me a sense of discipline, and when very early one morning on Victoria Embankment, by Charing Cross railway bridge, I saw an airman – hatless and looking over the embankment at the River Thames – I moved in to ask why. He was evasive. So I asked to see his pass… no pass. He was absent without leave, so I took him to Cannon Row, from where the RAF Police could be called from their base in Kensington. In the station he pulled out a Luger automatic pistol, causing the Station Officer and me to react quickly to take it from him. The pistol had a full magazine and a bullet in the breach. We put him in a cell minus gun, belt and boots, but what happened next caused a flurry of activity. He was allowed to keep his spectacles but, having removed them and broken a lens, he cut his wrists in order to lose blood. Eventually he appeared before Bertram Rees, the Bow Street magistrate, who agreed he should be handed over to the Royal Air Force; and thus ended the incident, except to say that the Station Officer was the formidable disciplinarian James Starritt, 6 ft 4 in., ex-captain Royal Marines Provost Branch, who went on to be knighted as Deputy

Commissioner. For court, I had learned my evidence by heart but mistakenly called the Luger a 'revolver', which incurred the military wrath of respected Station Sergeant Starritt, standing behind me, whose stage whisper, '*It's a pistol, not a revolver!*' could be heard by everyone. I was red-faced. I hope the airman got some help, but in military terms he had a lot to answer, including where he acquired the gun. There were many legendary tales about James Starritt, an exceptional policeman, who on this occasion had conscientiously accompanied me to court.

In the mid-1960s, as staff officer to Sir Arthur Young at the Police Extended Interview Boards held at Eastbourne, I again met James Starritt, who was observing the procedures, and we reminisced in a relaxed way about past 'characters' at Cannon Row and events in the early 1950s.

Trafalgar Square

In the 1950s, demand for cameras and films had still not been satisfied due to the war years' shortages, thereby enabling street photographers to make huge profits. Tourists were targets, and there were plenty of them in London for the 1951 Festival of Britain on the South Bank. They were promised large group photographs to be sent to their homes. A charge of £5 was normal (this was a lot of money in the 1950s). The victims/witnesses were mostly from the United States or Canada, but when the photographs did not arrive very few complained. However, some did complain, and we tried to prevent this illegal trade – which in any case was contrary to the Trafalgar Square Act, 1952. There was no power of arrest, so the game was to see them take a photograph, stop the accused, tell them they would be reported for illegal trading and note their replies. We already knew the culprits' names and addresses. I saw the Chief Inspector at Cannon Row, getting his permission to spend three weeks at the Square with a colleague, and foregoing refreshment breaks in the police station. (We took some food to the police box on site and discreetly ate in there.) During a normal refreshment break at the police station one would first eat, then write up reports. The street photographers would know our whereabouts and could, in that short time, make more money than I was earning in a month. By our staying on post they dare not work at all.

On one occasion we arranged with colleagues from Bow Street to assist by stopping the photographers as they exited the Strand doors of the then Charing Cross post office; meanwhile we would chase them to the Duncannon Street entrance. Trying to evade us, the photographers duly fled the Square to emerge in the Strand, but alas, when we got to the Strand, the Bow Street police had stopped the wrong people, who were amazed to be told they had acted illegally! We 'dusted them down' and tendered apologies. This cat-and-mouse activity, a war of attrition, continued until the photographers gave up. But it did not end there. I went on holiday to Torquay, Devon, and from there visited the Royal Show at Newton Abbot. Who should be there but all the Trafalgar Square photographers. There were cries of 'Oh, no!' when they saw me, but they had the grace to laugh, and so did I! There was no ill feeling.

Camera Thief

One plausible thief preyed on Trafalgar Square/Buckingham Palace tourists carrying cameras. He would engage them in conversation and had a good knowledge of camera value. Next, he offered a good sum of stated cash for their cameras, taking his victims to a 'camera shop' in the Strand. Getting them to wait outside, he went into Boots Chemists in Trafalgar House with their cameras, and out of Boots' side exit into the arcade, never to be seen again. So many complaints were received that a team of young policemen was brought out in plain clothes with a brief to watch any man answering the description who approached tourists with cameras. We watched the crowds, made many 'stops', never found the prime suspect, but saw other crimes being committed and basked in the glory of the arrests and results. Strangely, the camera incidents stopped.

Downing Street

After a summit meeting on an American battleship, Prime Minister Winston Churchill returned to Downing Street after midnight. I was on duty outside with a colleague. Next, the Prime Minister's Special Branch detective came out of No. 10 to see who else was about in the street; it was absolutely quiet. 'What happens next,' he said, 'the press must not know.' And they did not get to hear. The Russian Ambassador had been called and entered No. 10 at well after midnight. It was never reported, and I felt good about that, though I would have loved to know what had been said within at the height of the so-called 'cold war'. I doubt if such secrecy could be maintained in present days, when the press seem to be permanently in situ.

One night outside No. 10 we were on duty when a black Humber car came up the street at speed. In a split second we assumed it was a police senior officer coming to inspect, and my colleague, Constable Ben Redhead, stepped forward prepared to salute, until the speed of the car did not slacken. It carried on past us and went down the Foreign Office steps. There are two flights of steps. It hit the flat area after the first set of steps and nearly somersaulted, but as the back wheels crashed back on the steps it freed the front of the car, which then bounced to the bottom of the second flight, to disappear at speed into St James's Park. It had been chased by a police Wolseley car, which wrongly thought the Humber would be trapped in the cul-de-sac. It got away, but Ben Redhead was able to telephone the registration number directly from the front number plate, which was left on the Foreign Office steps.

Camaraderie

Night duty for three consecutive weeks was strangely relaxing, and it came round quickly, followed by six weeks on 'days'. In the summer, however, we missed the clean, fresh air, and organised day trips to the coast. Reduced rail fares could be obtained, provided one travelled before seven o'clock in the morning. Off duty by six o'clock, we returned to the police 'Section House' (120 single men stayed there), hurriedly took some refreshment, then a dozen of us would travel with a cheap day return from Victoria to Brighton.

Several hours would be spent sleeping on the beach, followed by a swim, then a visit to the Hove cricket ground to watch, for example, Sussex play Surrey. It was lovely to sit in the sun, breathe fresh air and appreciate the skills of the Bedser brothers,

Peter May, Ken Suttle and others. Following one more swim, we would then return to Victoria and prepare to go back on duty at 9.45 p.m. By the early hours of the next morning it took a lot of willpower to stay alert. One method in Downing Street, and also Westminster Abbey, was to thread the issue leather belt round the railings then resecure it round the waist. With one's body fixed erect to the railings it made standing just a little easier, and strangely we were extra alert to avoid being caught! A refinement of this was to place the truncheon up the sleeve and hold it in position in the cupped hand. If one momentarily dozed off, the hand would relax and the truncheon would fall to the ground, causing immediate consciousness! This dubious activity would be irresponsible in today's heightened security. Night-duty leather belts ceased to be issued.

The Chief Superintendent

Chief Superintendent Osborne was in charge of 'A' Division, which covered the Royal Palaces, Hyde Park, Green Park, St James's Park, the Houses of Parliament and most of the government offices, and stretched to Victoria and Vauxhall Bridge: quite a responsibility. Ex-Royal Navy, he wore the ribbons of the two World Wars and lived on the Division at Rochester Row. He was very conscientious, and late at night would sometimes send for his car with the intention of visiting most of the protection posts. Even on Christmas Day we expected his visit, this time to wish us well. One evening he telephoned the switchboard at Cannon Row asking for extension 13 – the garage. This triggered the usual activity; all the posts, including Buckingham Palace, Downing Street, Clarence and York House to Wellington Arch were alerted. He was respectfully saluted during his visits and no doubt went late to bed well satisfied that everything was in order – it was! However, one similar evening the 'alert' message was sent to Clarence House, where the public line used by police was permanently connected to the police lodge situated by Stable Yard Road. Royal residents at the time were Princess Elizabeth and the Duke of Edinburgh. The Duke was sitting at the switchboard on the first floor, making a call, when he saw the yellow discs flutter on the lodge police line. He took the call. He next opened the window and called to the police lodge, 'It means nothing to me, but it might mean something to you: "Codseyes is on the ground." '

Brumas

At London Zoo a brown bear had given birth and the new cub was called Brumas, attracting a lot of publicity and a large influx of welcome visitors. At the same time, a new police recruit joined us from Leicester, occupying a room in the single men's quarters. It was soon noticed that his back and chest were unusually hairy and he was promptly called 'Brumas', a nickname he accepted in good spirit. Brumas became involved with an accident at Trafalgar Square. Briefly, a Rolls-Royce motor car was parked outside South Africa House when a milk float, with a heavy liquid load, rolled down the hill to collide with the rear of the Rolls, doing much damage. The milkman/driver was prosecuted for failing to set the handbrake and the case was heard at Bow Street Magistrates' Court. Brumas gave his evidence but omitted to say why the float had rolled forward – the omitted downhill slope of the road being a critical factor. The magistrate asked, 'Officer, is this on the level?'

'Oh yes,' replied Brumas. 'Straight up, Your Worship.'

I was not there, but the court is said to have collapsed with laughter. I remember his true name well, simply because of this incident. It was the talk of the canteen.

The Coronation of HM Queen Elizabeth II

At East Lane School, North Wembley, I was very lucky to experience dedicated and skilled teachers whom I wished to please. Much emphasis was given to handwriting. We had to write daily in our best 'hand' the complete alphabet plus the numerals 1 to 9 and 0. This became a heading and was duly inspected. If approved, then all the writing on the remainder of that page had to be of the same standard as the heading – or rewritten. The sloping angle of the upward and downward strokes and loops had to be precise and the letters 't' and 'd', for example, had to be slightly smaller in height than the 'l' or 'h'. All in all it was good training, and the result of this was that I left school able to write accurately at speed and, more slowly, to a copperplate standard.

On 6 February 1952, HM King George VI died in his sleep and his daughter flew back from Kenya to be proclaimed Queen Elizabeth II. It was a shock to the people of the nation, who remembered the King with affection as the Head of State in the recent war. At the funeral there was a two minutes' silence, signalled by a gun on Horse Guards Parade, and a sudden utter silence when the traffic stopped; taxi and bus drivers alighted from their vehicles to stand to attention and the birds from St James's Park, Trafalgar Square and the River Thames took to the sky in fright. Prime Minister Winston Churchill paid a moving tribute to His Majesty's courage in peace and war.

I was later booking in for refreshment at Cannon Row, to be told by the Station Officer that the Divisional Plan-Drawer wished to see me. Puzzled, I duly went to see him. He told me that a survey of handwriting of personnel had been undertaken and my handwriting made me the prime candidate to assist him draw plans of Westminster, on which the police planning of the Coronation of HM The Queen would be based. I readily accepted. What an offer! There was the added bonus of being taken off night duty, on which I always had a feeling of being 'jet-lagged', though that expression was not known in the 1950s.

So I set about helping Police Constable 606'A' James Brown, a 6 ft 6 in. tall, gentle giant of a man, who had joined the police in the 1930s during the general depression and General Strike. A qualified mine surveyor from Houghton-le-Spring, County Durham, he matriculated at age fifteen and had the ability and skill to draw accurate plans for court and traffic planning. I helped him measure the whole route of the Coronation procession, which was to embrace a lot of Westminster, the Royal Parks, Oxford Street, Regent Street, Piccadilly, Trafalgar Square, Northumberland Avenue and the Thames Embankment to Westminster Abbey. There was a 'forward' route and a 'return' route, all of which was to be drawn to a scale of eighty-eight feet to one inch. Every street had a printed road width with a stated distance from building to building. On this plan, decisions were based about removal of traffic islands (to facilitate progress of the royal procession, massed bands et cetera), crush barriers (temporary and permanent), first-aid posts, refreshment tents, viewing stands, toilets, temporary fire-brigade posts, and the positioning of police who would arrive from all over the United Kingdom. A tented camp for police was to be erected in Kensington Gardens and west of Hyde Park. All Ordnance Survey maps were pre-war and out of date, so we had much to do. I learned triangulation methods and conscientiously penned all street and building names in block capitals.

We checked our tapes for accuracy on the brass standard measurements embedded in the stonework at Trafalgar Square. Standards like chains, rod, pole and perch – still there in brass – are no longer used. As a matter of interest, there is another standard set of measurements in Guildhall, City of London. Both venues are also updated for metric measurement and accuracy is tested at 60° Fahrenheit. Just inch perfect was good enough for us, for we measured in all weathers.

The whole police operation was eventually based on Jim Brown's meticulous plans, which were reproduced, cut up and distributed to sector commanders so that all concerned knew the precise location of their responsibility. The fire brigade, St John Ambulance, Ministry of Works and voluntary services were given copies of the area affecting their personnel. The overall plan was huge, measuring approximately four metres long by three metres high. Jim Brown was rightly proud of it.

Coronation Day, 2 June 1953, duly arrived and Jim Brown and I reported for duty at 3.30 a.m. outside Westminster Abbey, a sort of reward for our work on the plans. Outside the Abbey we were very impressed with the cadets of the Royal Military Academy, Sandhurst, who lined the route under the command of Major Hedley-Dent, who regularly patrolled close behind the cadets, giving encouragement and support during the very long hours. It poured with rain and the cadets on the Abbey side of the road were ordered to step back under the erected cloth canopy for protection – a good move until the order 'Present arms!', when the bayonets punctured the canopy and some collected rain came through!

After the great day passed, there was a failure of communication between New Scotland Yard Traffic Branch and 'A' Division Headquarters at Cannon Row. Jim Brown was on the roll of Cannon Row. The Coronation procession was planned by Traffic Branch: each thought the other would ensure that Jim Brown would get a Coronation Medal for his work, but neither checked, and his name did not get on the list. However, the unpopular civilian canteen manager at Cannon Row was duly rewarded. This upset the troops, and Jim Brown missed out. The jungle telegraph, as it is called, was very unhappy.

I repeat, as it's of interest, a wartime story told to me by Jim Brown. Night fighter-pilots, flying over the St James/Whitehall area, reported to the Air Ministry that a flashing light occurred with regularity, and an enquiry was suggested in case the 'signals' were deliberate: the whole area was extremely sensitive. When most had gone to air-raid shelters, Jim Brown and another Cannon Row stalwart, Constable Jim Nevett, went in the other direction, upwards in the Duke of York Statue* in The Mall and the Wellington Arch at Hyde Park Corner respectively. (In a

---

* The Duke of York was the second son of George III. His column was paid for by deducting a day's pay from all members of the British Army. Legend has it that he owed money in the West End and therefore his back was to that direction. There is a staircase within the statue.

blackout there was no background light from shops or traffic lights, no office or street lighting – just complete blackness, possibly relieved by the moon.) Armed with Meccano and wingnuts, they erected basic direction recording equipment and waited for an air raid, which duly came. Planes were heard overhead, and sure enough there was the flashing to the sky; sightings were taken. Next day in daylight, lines were noted from the fixings, and when applied to a map they crossed at the Athenaeum Club, Pall Mall. This was odd; the Prime Minister and the Archbishop of Canterbury were members! Enquiries revealed that when planes were heard overhead, the hall porters would call the members to take cover and they went to the basement by lift. It was the lift mechanism on the roof which flashed to the sky.

This is all related because for me, at twenty-three years old, the Coronation map-making was an extraordinary experience, brought about solely because I paid attention to the teachers at school over ten years previously. There are not many occupations-within-occupations where handwriting skill is critical: this was one of them.

After the Coronation, Jim Brown took some leave and I returned to street duty. I was soon called back to help the Flying Squad, who had been involved in a shooting incident in Hyde Park and Mayfair. Normally Jim Brown would have handled the plan preparations with ease, but in this case, where plans were urgently required, I was the only person who had received the benefit of Jim Brown's training and thus responded to the call. Briefly, there had been an armed robbery in a jewellery shop in Kensington. Witnesses had notified 999 with the registration number of the getaway car, and this number was promptly broadcast to all cars (no personal radios for beat patrols in those days). By sheer fortunate coincidence, a Flying Squad car was stationary in Kensington Gore in heavy traffic, by the entrance to Hyde Park, when they realised the wanted car was just ahead of them. The robbers also realised they had been spotted and turned into Hyde Park along the West Carriageway, then along the North Carriageway (parallel with Bayswater Road), finally turning south into Park Lane and exiting Hyde Park into Mayfair.

During this hairy pursuit, shots were fired at the police Rover car and several penetrated the windscreen. When the criminals decamped from their car in Mayfair, more shots were fired and a police motorcyclist had to take refuge behind a pillar postbox. This was a big event in police terms, and plans were needed urgently for Marlborough Street Magistrates' Court and subsequently a possible trial.

Luckily, Jim Brown and I had measured most of the Hyde Park carriageways for the Coronation and I was able to carefully copy and accurately draw the material route up to Mayfair, which was not on Cannon Row Division, but on 'C' Division, West End Central police station. The 'C' Division Plan-Drawer could not help, so I measured and drew the locus of the Mayfair shooting, including the pillar box, and relied on pre-war Ordnance Survey for the basic layout.

On the day of the court hearing I reattended the scene, cycling round Hyde Park, checking and noting, because one could never be sure what question the lawyers would ask. In Mayfair I stood at the pillar box to memorise the scene, and to my horror realised that I had included a street which was no longer there. I was somewhat stressed about this and, after taking the oath, I told the Court that the plans of Hyde Park were drawn to scale and the enlarged plan of Mayfair was also drawn to scale. I omitted the usual words 'correct and' (drawn to scale). If counsel for either side raised the error I would have apologised and explained, but to my relief, though the plans were well used and referred to in court, no one noticed the extra Mayfair street, which had since been built over, and I was very relieved!

The skills I learned through assisting the preparations for HM Coronation were very useful.

Bishopsgate Stories

I went to Bishopsgate police station as an Inspector in 1963. Bishopsgate is opposite Liverpool Street railway station and regarded as the busiest police station in the City. The railway station brought in a lot of work, as did Petticoat Lane on Sunday, where we were responsible for the City side; its proper name is Middlesex Street.

Tower Bridge

When on night duty I tried to visit every one of the constables on the street, and the longest walk was up to Tower Bridge. It became routine for the bridge constable, on seeing the Duty Inspector walking towards the bascules, to walk to meet him to save the last one hundred yards. On this occasion I could not even see the officer, Constable Eric Bly (ex-Welsh Guards and a cricketer). So I carried on walking, reaching the centre of the bridge where I saw Eric Bly leaning over the bascules and not moving. He's ill, I thought, and quickened my pace. When I got to him I found he was holding on to a man who had tried to jump into the Thames. Together we dragged him back to the walkway, whereupon he tried to jump again. We sent for transport and, as he was under the influence of drink, called the police doctor to see him and to advise us. It transpired that he was bitterly disappointed that his football team (Chelsea, as I recall) had lost in the FA Cup semi-final; and the drink had obviously affected his mind, for within a week he revisited Tower Bridge and jumped off. This time his body was found one week later. A waste of a life.

As a lad I was familiar with the shipping in the Pool of London, and the movement at the local wharves, viewed from Tower Bridge, was worth watching. The dockers unloaded into barges and the busy tugs towed the cargoes further upriver. It was an active scene. One New Year's Eve I timed my walk to meet the constable posted to Tower Bridge so it would actually be midnight when we stood together in the middle of the bridge. It was a moving occasion. The sirens of the ships in the Pool of London started and, as if echoing, the sirens of the ships towards Greenwich and Gravesend carried on the New Year message, a real cacophony of sound on a very still night, which I shall never forget. With the absence of ships in the Thames today, it will never be repeated. I wished the constable a Happy New Year, shook his hand and carried on with the patrol.

Corruption

Having looked up the word 'corruption' in the dictionary, I reckon it will fit what I write about next. In any group of one hundred people there will be those at the top end who have been well brought up, honest, will not wrongfully use the office telephone, will not go sick and will be well motivated to do a good job of work. At the lower end of the one hundred are those who will be late for work (and usually the first to leave), reporting frequent sickness, are generally lazy and requiring constant supervision. A skill of management is to lead the middle group, who can be influenced either way, into the correct and honest way of everyday dealing. If, however, a manager leads his staff into dishonesty, then he should receive treble punishment and retribution for the betrayal of trust which can so affect the lives of others.

An Inspector on night duty in the City was responsible to the Superintendent for police activity during a tour of duty. To assist the Inspector were three sergeants and about twelve constables, one sergeant being virtually desk-bound in the station. I used to patrol the Division with each sergeant responsible for the constables in his area, and generally visit the 'troops': this was routine. The said troops expected to see the Inspector and feel supported.

One night the police radio reported a shop-breaking round the back of Throgmorton Street. I attended with a sergeant to find the patrol van with a crew already there waiting for me. A tobacconist's shop window had a huge hole in the middle and a brick now in the display, which had in turn collapsed boxes of cigars and cigarettes. I got involved, collected some small cigars from the bottom of the window and was very pleased that they fitted perfectly into their box. I then arranged that the window should be cleared, pasted up with brown paper to lessen danger (a service we provided), and the goods to be secured in the police station. Having done that, I continued the patrol, returning to Bishopsgate.

After breakfast I asked to see the property and checked it against the 'Found property book'. Alas, there was no box of small cigars. I sent for the van sergeant and said, 'There are cigars missing from this property. I know that for a fact. Go back to the scene with your crew, check behind the bins and check in the van. If these cigars are not here within fifteen minutes my next telephone call will be to the Detective Chief Inspector.' He left, rather pale, returning in ten minutes with three boxes of cigars. I gave the crew what is known as the 'Angel's warning' – never do that again. I relate this because one of those involved in this incident was subsequently arrested and went to prison for a similar reason in the next sad story. He was well out of the Force.

I was Duty Officer when Securicor telephoned to report a shop-breaking in Fenchurch Street. I attended the scene. There was a large construction site, and steel scaffolding surrounded the tall office block then under construction. It was the job of Securicor to visit the site with keys and check that all was well. All was not well, for neatly hanging on the scaffolding were hundreds of suits, trousers and equipment ready to be loaded into a lorry which had been seen to decamp. Rain was imminent. The thieves had gained access into the rear of Austin Reed, the outfitters, by using an electric saw to cut a large hole in the rear door, leaving the alarm contacts in place. (Passive infrared detectors had not yet been installed.)

I sent for the van, which patrolled the City with a sergeant and four crew, and we loaded the stolen goods using 'five-bar gate' methods of accounting for trousers, belts, jackets et cetera. The whole lot was taken to Bishopsgate police station and there placed on clothing racks from our store, locked in a cell, and the paperwork completed. This was routine, not really a story, just an insecurity dealt with properly. However, when I had left the Force I saw a press headline, 'City Police arrested for theft'. I bought the paper, read it on the spot and felt very sad and sorry, for I knew all the men concerned, who were basically good workers. Austin Reed – the same shop as in the previous story – had been found insecure in the night. The Inspector (who also went to prison) attended, called the van and invited the crew to sort out clothing for themselves – which some did, thus betraying the very reason for their employment. Their homes were searched and the property recovered. Prosecutions followed. The loss of job, stress for their families and general disgrace was a high price for clothing, but illustrates the point that middle management has a big responsibility for standards and guidance.

The Three-Card Trick Man

Every front office had a charity box – usually for the City of London and Metropolitan Police Widows and Orphans – and this box was used by those grateful for police services such as restoration of property, lost children or dogs. But I was pleased no one was watching when a 'donation' was passed to me by a 'three-card trick man' I was bailing to appear in court. He had been arrested in Middlesex Street and detained for a couple of hours until the close of the market. The trickster's method was to deal cards on a box and invite members of the public to 'pick the lady' – the queen. First, with some cooperation from associates, the public would see what they thought were other members of the public winning cash by spotting the said lady. Next they would have a go themselves, and might be allowed to win. Once punters became interested, the stakes would be raised and if, for example, there was too much money on a card which the associates knew was the 'queen', a call of 'Police!' would cause the box, cards and money to be snatched and the gamers would run off, leaving the poor (foolish) punters minus their stake. In any case it was illegal. I had charged this particular man and was returning 'Property found on person', which is different to 'Property subject of the charge'; that is retained for court and possibly forfeit. He seemed very pleased that I was returning £147 found in his back pocket, and on leaving the charge room he deftly flicked a five-pound note into the open charge desk drawer. That was a 'first', and he left instantly. It occurred to me afterwards that he had expected me also to put his £147 as 'Property subject of the charge' and felt he had made a profit! At least we had stopped his operations on this Sunday morning.

An Emotional Moment

British Transport Police from Liverpool Street station arrived one afternoon with a very young fair-haired lad who had escaped from an approved school. He was polite, alert, clean and cooperative. I did not ask him why he was in the approved school – maybe I should have done – but he said he did not like it there. We duly contacted the approved school and they arranged to send an escort, estimated time of arrival two hours. This was in the days when escapees were caned on their return and it occurred to me that he was in for a lot of pain. We fed him and he asked to speak to me from the detention room – we had not placed him in a cell. He requested a 'great favour', so I asked him what he proposed. He simply wanted to speak to his mother on the telephone. I agreed, provided he first wrote down the telephone number, then allowed me to dial it and speak, to confirm it was his mother. It was his mother. The conversation he then had was so affectionate, warm and fluent that I could not stay in the room – I was deeply moved. He was very appreciative.

The escort duly arrived and he was taken away. I often wondered what happened to that lad and felt sure there was a better place for him than a caning in an approved school. I saw pictures in *The Times* of prisoners in a young offenders' institute where their buttocks had been caned and the flesh cut and bruised. This caused me to shift my opinion. Though some thugs deserve caning, it is an unsuitable punishment which can be abused. As I write this, I also consider that one reason why there is not a graffiti problem in Singapore is because culprits will be automatically caned. In the west of England vandals have, I now read, urinated in fresh water bowsers placed in streets for use of the public during their interrupted water supply. Would a deserved caning be in order? Vandals abuse a tolerant society.

Drunks and White Gloves

Some nights at Bishopsgate were so busy that I was pleased to get home and slump into bed. One particular night I remember having charged fourteen men: drunks, drunken drivers, six youths causing criminal damage at roadworks, two assaults and one car thief.

I learned to be careful and wary of drunks. One morning I handed over the prisoners, yet to be bailed, to the early turn, Inspector Geoff Lorton, who luckily was a skilled first-aider and leading member of the City Police first-aid team. A paralytic drunk had been brought in by four officers, each one holding a limb. I recalled the framed definition of drunkenness which used to hang in the bar of the National Provincial Bank Rowing Club at Hammersmith.

> He is not drunk who from the floor can rise and drink and ask for more. But he is drunk who prostrate lies without the power to drink or rise.

Absolutely drunk, and fitting the quoted definition, our man was placed in a cell – laces, boots and belt removed – to be charged when he was sober and could understand what was being said. I was long home and in bed when Geoff Lorton telephoned. He just thought I ought to know that when the drunk was sober he complained of a pain in his leg, which turned out to be a fractured femur, the largest bone in the body. Geoff Lorton had dealt with it and the prisoner was in St Bartholomew's Hospital. I thanked him.

I have been to West End Central, where the Duty Officer, taking charges, has been crazily busy. To West End Central, fourteen charges at Bishopsgate would be a quiet night! People cause pressure in police stations and hospitals. I have also known some days, usually after Christmas, when there have been no cases at the Guildhall or Mansion House courts, in which case the presiding magistrate would be presented with a pair of white gloves by the Clerk of the Court, a City tradition.

Snow Hill Stories

St Paul's Cathedral (1)

I was Acting Inspector on night duty in the autumn of 1962. Acting Inspectors were known throughout the Force as 'TNBs', short for 'Toffee-nosed Bastards', for it was thought TNBs were invariably strict on discipline whilst in line for promotion to full Inspector. They were reputed not to take chances or run the risk of incurring the Superintendent's wrath, for this could affect prospects of promotion. I tried hard not to enhance the continuance of this general reputation.

At about one o'clock in the morning we were looking forward to some respite, as the first few hours of night duty had been hectic due to exceptional gale-force winds which had set off alarms, blown down hoardings, damaged windows and displaced roadworks signs. A man in a state of collapse suddenly staggered into the front office of Snow Hill. He sat down to recover his breath and after several attempts blurted out that St Paul's Cathedral scaffolding – up to the top of the dome – was going to collapse. St Paul's Cathedral to the top of the cross is 365 feet high. He had run all the way from the cathedral with the news, about 800 yards, no doubt wishing he had been fitter.

We rushed out to St Paul's and, sure enough, there was immense danger. The stone cleaners had left tarpaulins tied to the scaffolding and the effect was that it looked like a massive galleon in full sail, causing the scaffolding to buckle. Illuminated from below by floodlighting, scaffold boards were becoming airborne from the Golden Ball level, high above the dome, then crashing to earth. While assessing the situation, we watched one board flutter down from the top to break a cast-iron spike off the decorative garden railings, while other boards fell into the roadway.

We immediately diverted traffic, sending for the contractors. To their credit, by 2.30 a.m. a team, with knives, arrived to climb the scaffolding and free the gigantic sails. With the tarpaulins eventually cut away they declared the scaffolding safe. 'If it was going to come down, guv'nor, it would have done so while the sheets were there.'

That sounded very logical, but I was doubtful, for I knew a brick wall is safe only when absolutely vertical and so, before traffic was to be released, opted to get confirmation from the City of London's dangerous-structures surveyor. He unfortunately lived at Brighton and would not attend until daylight. Road closures also required notification to the fire and ambulance services and to passenger transport operators. It was a key route for Fleet Street newspaper vans with train deadlines at Liverpool Street and Fenchurch Street railway stations.

I handed over to the 'early turn' Inspector at six o'clock, went off duty and to bed that morning, fearing for the traffic chaos of the rush hour and knowing one of two things would happen:

a)   I would be ridiculed for keeping Ludgate Hill shut if the surveyor backed the contractors, or

b)   I would have been judged to have done the right thing.

Luckily option b) was agreed, and Ludgate Hill stayed shut for over a week while many miles of buckled scaffolding were dismantled and made safe. I winced at the cost but survived.

St Paul's Cathedral (2)

This story is shorter but still set in the early 1960s. City Police cadets, led by experienced instructor Constable Jock Watt (ex-Scots Guards) visited St Paul's and climbed to the Golden Ball level. In the floor there is a thick glass panel through which one can look down to see the wonderful black and white compass design on the cathedral floor below. In answer to a question, the verger/guide foolishly announced that the glass was unbreakable and invited a cadet to jump on it to test his claim. A cadet with steel-tipped boots duly tried, cracked the glass and went through up to his hips. He promptly fainted. Just imagine the scene below, the heavy glass appearing as from heaven and shattering amongst visitors! The beloved City of London Police got away with that one, but an injury or fatality would have been highly publicised. That was close!

St Paul's Cathedral (3)

President John F Kennedy of the United States of America was assassinated by a rifle bullet on 12 November 1963. It was momentous news. There followed a memorial service at St Paul's Cathedral on a Saturday, at which many heads of state, military and VIPs were to attend. Our leave was cancelled and the City Police was out in force to line the City route. I was in a group of about twenty police to assemble halfway up Ludgate Hill. There were still wartime bomb sites about at the rear of a Ludgate Hill jeweller's shop. We had no idea that shopbreakers had spent all Friday night digging and excavating underneath the building in order to come up from below into the jeweller's shop. You can guess the villains' feelings when they looked out to see so many City Police outside the shop! They decamped, but their hard work was not discovered until Monday when the City returned to work. If only we had known…

St Paul's Cathedral (4)

Dwight D Eisenhower was a five-star general of the United States Army, who later became the thirty-fourth president of the United States of America. As a lad I was much in awe of his responsibility as Supreme Commander of the Allied Forces in Europe, charged with the task of planning and supervising the successful invasion of France and Germany in 1944–1945. Later in 1951 he was the first supreme commander of NATO.

For me the 1939–1945 war had been a huge geography lesson as I read daily of the worldwide battles and followed newspaper maps of defeats and successes. General 'Dee' Eisenhower was, to my young mind, on a par with HM King George and Winston Churchill as a key leader to deliver victory in Europe.

President Eisenhower visited London in 1961 and I spoke nine critical words to him in the following circumstances. He was attending St Paul's Cathedral to pay respects to a memorial for fallen soldiers, sailors and airmen, and my role, at the conclusion of this visit, was security at the south side door of the cathedral from where he was due to exit.

The President brought huge international press interest and pressmen, transported in a chartered London Transport bus, followed his every move. Before the President's party came out through the side exit I realised that the rarely used heavy steel trellis, which normally secured that area, was pushed back, but the immovable steel rail on which the trellis wheels ran was still down and due to provide a trip-rail hazard for the President. To complicate matters, the President's style on this visit was to repeatedly look up and raise both arms above his head in the form of a salute to the Press corps. In cricket parlance, everywhere he went he was signalling a 'six'.

As President Eisenhower got to the steel rail he was virtually next to me. I said, 'Mr President, please be careful of that rail, sir.' He turned to me; then, surprised, looked down, saw the rail and thanked me. I have since wondered what would have happened if he had fallen: it would have been a tragedy making international news, for there were steep stone steps ahead.

Accidental Deaths

In 1963 King Baudouin of Belgium paid a state visit to London. Normally, similar visits would commence with HM The Queen receiving guests at Victoria Station, for a state drive to Buckingham Palace via Parliament Square, Whitehall and The Mall. This visit was different: the royal party was to come to the River Thames in a Royal Navy ship, then transfer to a launch for Westminster Pier, where they would be officially received.

It made good sense, from security and safety aspects, for Thames bridges to be manned by police to prevent a handbag, or worse, being dropped onto the royal launch below.

Then a sergeant, I was detailed to attend Blackfriars Bridge with four constables. Our brief was to keep the centre arch clear of pedestrians until the royal launch had safely passed. Similar arrangements had been made for all the Thames bridges up to Westminster.

The royal launch had just come into sight, having cleared Southwark Bridge, when a young man came running up to me and said, 'Can you please come? My mate has hung himself.'

A death of any sort is serious, so I could not delegate this one. I handed over the royal duty to the constables and hurriedly accompanied the young man to the Blackfriars underpass building site. Sure enough, his 'mate' had hanged himself, using rope tied to the site office ceiling conduit piping. His naked body had been cut down by colleagues and an electric fire, left on all night, had caused an unpleasant atmosphere. A chair was nearby.

I sent for the police doctor, the CID and the duty officer. A photographer with forensic officers also arrived. On the face of it, here was a man who had simply committed suicide. The body was removed and everyone eventually departed, so I was left to make site enquiries and write the report as the first police officer at the scene.

It is always important in cases like this to trace the last person spoken to by the deceased. I discovered from his building work colleagues that he intended to go home to the West Country during the next weekend. Further, he had the previous day bought a portable radio: we found the receipt and, in the office waste-paper basket, draft typewritten copies of letters to his home. All concerned were surprised that he had committed suicide. Then came a critical revelation: the first workman on the scene had removed many photographs with sexual connotations. I took possession of them and felt for the family, who had not yet been informed. I momentarily considered if I could protect them from the knowledge of the explicit photographs – the simple way being to throw the lot in the coke boiler at Snow Hill. That would have been unprofessional and a big mistake, possibly affecting any insurance considerations. I declared the whole and the Coroner for the City of London, with a jury, found for accidental death. It was not a suicide. This attempt by the deceased to induce a strange sexual experience caused his demise.

And the King of Belgium got safely to Westminster.

Window cleaners are at risk and they take chances, lean too far and, by overbalancing, can pay a heavy price. The window cleaner at a Holborn Viaduct building was suspended in a specially erected fibreglass cradle seat, allowing him to use pulleys to access all the windows. Unfortunately the end-stop clamp on the girder overhanging the top of this building became loose, the wheels came off the end and he fell about one hundred feet, dying instantly from injuries. We did what we could at the scene. At the inquest, the Coroner called the supervisor of the window cleaning company to explain how window cleaning cradles were tested. The supervisor said that to test he simply got into the cradle, stood up, then banged the pulley wheels against the end-stop. 'What happens if the end-stop is loose?' asked the Coroner.

'Well, the wheels come off and I go down,' was the reply. There was restrained laughter in court and even the Coroner smiled, but it was a tragedy for the family.

Fleet Building, Farringdon Street

When travelling to duty at Smithfield Market, always a scene of intense activity, I boarded the weekday 5 a.m. train from Petts Wood, which conveniently went straight to Holborn Viaduct (no longer an option) in good time for 5.45 muster. I got to know the fellow passengers who boarded along the route; they were print workers, market workers and one man from Beckenham, who was the head plumber at the huge Fleet Building in Farringdon Street. They were relaxed, lovely people, sometimes exchanging allotment produce as the journey progressed. One morning on the train, our plumber gently complained to me that he had been arrested after engagement on a particularly nasty job attracting triple pay. The weekend night work consisted of wearing special protective clothing, using steel scouring bobbins on wire threaded through the waste pipes of the urinals in Fleet Building, then pulling 'to and fro' with a colleague until all pipes became freed from encrusted blockage. The pale-green powder, apparently excellent for allotments, was then collected in boxes. When leaving the building with two ammunition boxes, our plumber was stopped by police. You can guess the dialogue. 'What have you got there?' Reply: 'Two boxes of dried urine,' or words to that effect; enough to get anyone arrested. How the Station Officer dealt with that remained unrecorded.

March to Lambeth Palace

On a Sunday afternoon in early 1963, I reported for duty knowing there was to be a demonstration and march from the City into the Metropolitan Police area. The first job for the Duty Officer was to read through the diary and check the Special Orders for any unusual events. This march was to assemble in Smithfield Market. It would consist of workers from the industries of building, transport, markets, industry and commerce led by union leaders. The route would be Farringdon Street, Fleet Street, Strand, Trafalgar Square, Whitehall, Parliament Street, Victoria Embankment, Lambeth Bridge to the Archbishop's Palace at Lambeth, where the march would disperse and transport would bring us back to the City. Extra police had been allocated and at the border of the City – Fleet Street/Strand – where the Metropolitan Police would take over control. We were to stay with the march until the conclusion.

One assumed those taking part would have left-wing tendencies, but the extraordinary factor with this crowd was that they were marching in support of the policies of Enoch Powell MP, generally thought to be an intellectual right-wing Conservative, who had expressed strong views about immigration and repatriation. I introduced myself to the leader, telling him that it was the role of the City Police to progress the march safely along the approved City route. He was cooperative, very smart in a well-cut sports jacket with wide shoulders. He jumped onto a market barrow with a loud hailer to address the crowd, already several hundred strong and fast increasing.

Using the language of emphasis – slow, loud and with pauses for effect – his words were as follows.

'Brothers, we are gathered together this afternoon to demonstrate and show solidarity against the state of this country today. We are being overrun by immigrants. If your brothers who died for you in the war could see the state of this country they would cry...'

At that very moment it started to rain, as if the leader had a 'hot line' to heaven. There rose a huge cheer of support and, following more words, the march moved off in a good-humoured procession. It passed along the prescribed route peacefully, the

'Mets' took over at the Strand, and at the conclusion at the Archbishop's Palace they gave three cheers for the police!

I thought the overall event was bizarre; however, there was a repeat Sunday march a couple of months later when there was serious widespread disorder in Whitehall – maybe one of the first of the clashes between the National Front and the Socialist Workers' Party. I watched it on evening television in the comfort of home, whilst feeling sorry for the police on duty.

The Old Bailey Bomb, 8 March 1973

In the 1970s, London police had an exceptionally busy time dealing with bomb scares, some real, some made in good faith and others simply hoaxes. All were taken very seriously. Bombs in the City had already exploded, including the Bank of England and the nearby Tower of London. Also an Arab bomb had partly detonated in a local Jewish bank. The public were often delayed, due to false alerts, in railway stations, and I recall attending a deserted Liverpool Street Station – everyone had been evacuated, including shops – because it was reported that a suspicious-looking person had deposited a bomb in the Royal Mail postbox on the main station concourse. The Royal Mail understandably would not allow their employees to open suspect postboxes, so it was left to police to take action. Meanwhile, trains were backed up into Norfolk, Suffolk and Essex, the cost in lost time and confusion being enormous. Military bomb disposal officers attached to the police were in high demand, and to avoid further delays we simply opened the box with the Post Office keys, in the Liverpool Street case to find a roll of paper properly stamped and addressed.

A similar situation occurred in Fleet Street, when at peak newspaper production time the postbox outside the *Daily Telegraph* was the focus of attention. All traffic was diverted. Again we opened up to find a properly addressed packet. Many bomb calls were handled daily on what seemed to be a continuous basis.

On 8 March, the calls were so numerous that at Wood Street it was an 'all hands on deck' situation. I went out in a van to Throgmorton Street where there were two simultaneous bomb alerts, one in the street and the other in the Stock Exchange. Our crews were starting with a list and working through.

Two of many bomb alerts in Westminster dealt with by Metropolitan included one in Great Scotland Yard, which exploded, and one near New Scotland Yard, which was defused.

With this going on in the background, Londoner George Murrell (national service in the Royal Inniskilling Fusiliers), an Inspector at Snow Hill, prepared for 'late turn' duty as Duty Officer. He arrived early, having heard on the radio of the morning's bomb activity. Two suspect cars had been located in the City, one in Aldersgate Street (with which the 'early turn' Duty Officer was dealing) and the other in Old Bailey, opposite the Central Criminal Court. He went immediately to Old Bailey, where constables there indicated they had been unable to trace the driver and there had already been a fifteen-minute delay. George Murrell, a man of action, telephoned the Licensing Authority to find the reason for the delay. He was then told the delay was because the car was registered in Northern Ireland.

The following is taken from the George Murrell account of subsequent events, and I am grateful to him for permission to use an extract, and very respectful of his actions.

> This was enough for me. I immediately gave instructions to evacuate all buildings and people in the area, and with the PCs set about doing this. I went into the George Tavern asking the drinkers to leave, but being used to this sort of situation they showed no urgency. My response was to shout loudly, 'Well, if you are not going to get out I ****ing well am', and ran out of the door. They got the message and ran out after me. I then spotted a coach full of young schoolchildren stuck in stationary traffic in Fleet Lane. With assistance of their teachers I managed to get the children out, telling them to run down to take shelter under the railway bridge. Just as they got there the car bomb exploded. I was on the corner of Fleet Lane [by Old Bailey] about thirty yards away at the time. The force of the explosion threw me face down on the pavement, the blast lifting off my cap which travelled 100 yards... Miraculously I had escaped any injury and as I got to my feet I heard the noise of glass and other debris falling and the screams of persons injured.
>
> Looking round me I was horrified. There were people (including several of my PCs) nursing wounds. Every glass window in Hillgate House and other buildings had been blown out. The

entire side wall of the George public house had collapsed. A water main had burst and water was gushing into the street. Rubble and parts of damaged cars were everywhere, confusion reigned.

Looking Back
Private Memoirs of George Murrell

Prior to the explosion, the Metropolitan Police Bomb Squad having been alerted, ex-military bomb disposal officer, Major Biddle, was on his way in a police Land Rover. My brother, Robin, then Detective Chief Inspector at Snow Hill, hearing about the imminent arrival of the bomb disposal officer, went to walk past the suspect car to greet Major Biddle at the other end of Old Bailey in Ludgate Hill. Robin was stopped by Detective Constable Clive Buckland, a CID photographic officer, and advised not to go further. Robin was already a cricket-pitch distance from the suspect car and saw the Metropolitan Police vehicle turning into Old Bailey from Ludgate Hill when the suspect car exploded, causing injuries, damage and broken windows in a radius of several hundred yards, as described by George Murrell. Clive Buckland, now living in South Africa, undoubtedly saved Robin's life and they still keep in touch to this day.

A completely independent view is recorded in the book *You'll Go to London*[*], an autobiography of Lionel Ball of the London City Mission, who was the Force Chaplain. The following is reproduced with his kind permission.

Being in the right place at the right time is so important as I discovered on a March day in 1973. I had visited Police HQ in Old Jewry and was making my way up Cheapside when there was an explosion ahead of me. Within five minutes there was frantic police activity. My first inclination was to keep away and not indulge in the usual British tendency to be part of a gawping crowed and so hinder rescue services. On the other hand I wanted to be as much help as I could. I went immediately to Snow Hill Police Station and was welcomed by duty officers who

[*] Ball, Lionel, *You'll Go to London*, Christian Focus, 2008 (ISBN: 978-1-84550-314-7)

told me that a number of people, mostly policemen, had been injured. The IRA had planted a bomb outside the Central Criminal Court, the Old Bailey, and it had exploded causing considerable damage. I saw officers directing traffic and controlling crowds and some of them had torn uniforms and were nursing injuries. In the station I made sandwiches for the extra police personnel recalled for duty before making my way to St Bartholomew's Hospital. I visited twelve officers and a number of civilians. Two policemen were being operated on for serious injuries.

Robin was treated in St Bartholomew's Hospital for temporary deafness and cuts, and his suit was ruined. However, the large pockets in his trousers, unlike the rest of his suit, were of man-made fibre, which held the hot shrapnel. But for this he would have sustained injury in some sensitive places. Had the highly respected bomb disposal officer been thirty seconds earlier he too might have been killed. Many years later, Robin had tooth problems needing dental advice and an X-ray. The puzzled dentist telephoned Robin at work, asking that he attend the surgery as soon as possible. Wedged in his teeth below the eye was a fragment of the bomb – and it is still there to this day, medical advice being that it should not be disturbed!

The stained glass windows of nearby St Sepulchre's Church, protected in the war, had been blown out in 'peacetime' by the Irish Republican Army.

More Bomb Alerts

A well-known senior Northern Ireland politician used a Barbican flat, in the City of London, as his base, which was equipped with an intruder and attack alarm. We all knew that if this alarm activated there was to be swift action. As the City is known as 'The Square Mile', Wood Street police station being in the centre, a response to a burglar alarm in Barbican could be achieved in less than two minutes. I can recall many instances when responses had taken just thirty seconds. One night the politician's alarm activated and at the same time the Head Office of the Royal Mail, King Edward Building, near St Paul's Cathedral, reported that a 'bomb' was ticking in their building. I was the senior officer on duty and immediately thought there was an attack on the politician, with a 'diversion' bomb at King Edward Building, to split police activity. We hurriedly and anxiously attended both, which were false alarms: the politician had gone out for a drink, forgetting about his alarm (he was very apologetic) and the 'ticking bomb' was a battery operated child's washing machine, which had commenced a 'washing sequence' in the post.

Bomb alerts kept us very busy. They were difficult times, mostly originating from troubles in the United Kingdom, and one hopes that present pressures in the Middle East will not cause a return to those anxious days.

The Funeral of Sir Winston Spencer Churchill, Wartime Prime Minister

On 24 January 1965, Winston Churchill died and was accorded a State funeral. It was a major event, and the Grenadier Guards, who were to carry his coffin up the steps of St Paul's Cathedral, had been rehearsing at 5 a.m. for several days. Large crowds were expected.

Newly promoted, I had been transferred from Snow Hill to Bishopsgate 'C' Division, but on this day returned with many Bishopsgate colleagues to line the route outside St Paul's. It was a very cold day. Heads of State from innumerable countries were in attendance, many of them approaching on foot up Godliman Street to enter the side of the cathedral. When the funeral procession came up Ludgate Hill – the coffin on a gun carriage was hauled by the Royal Navy – the marching feet of the sailors grated on the sand which had been spread on the road. The steel wheels of the carriage crushed this sand, making an eerie sound which added to the tense, emotional atmosphere. Behind me in the crowd the public, listening to the BBC radio commentary on portable sets, heard words from his memorable wartime speeches, for example after Dunkirk:

> We shall not flag or fail. We shall go on to the end, we shall fight in France, we shall fight on the seas and oceans, we shall fight with growing confidence and growing strength in the air, we shall defend our Island whatever the cost, we shall fight on the landing

grounds, we shall fight in the fields and in the streets, we shall fight in the hills; we shall never surrender.

I had listened to these key speeches as a young lad – the Battle of Britain, the Blitz, North Africa, D-Day and finally VE day. The words came back to me, and I remembered being in Downing Street when he was Prime Minister. All this was so emotional that I felt benumbed; I hoped no one would ask a question or require a decision as the cortège went by. Thankfully, no one did. I have never experienced that feeling since and hope I never will. At times of high emotion I have heard that one should focus on something other than what is happening; this is more easily said than done.

Churchill quotation: 'The nation had the lion's heart. I had the luck to give the roar.'

St Bride's Church, Fleet Street

On the way to a recent (2007) Snow Hill reunion lunch at Ye Olde Cheshire Cheese in Fleet Street, my brother and I called at St Bride's Parish Church. The Francis family has a soft spot for this church, where our grandfather, then Police Constable John Abraham Francis, married Annie Deed on 9 August 1899. Both were residents of the parish – Bridewell Police Station and 4 Racquet Court, Fleet Street, respectively – and both addresses are now demolished.

When on the beat in 1962, I met the rector, the Reverend Dewi Morgan, who asked if arrangements could be made to keep a friendly eye on his daughters in the St Bride's vicarage nearby whilst he and his wife went on two weeks' holiday. I was so anxious to help that I neglected to ask the age of his daughters but duly entered the request in the 'parade book' at Snow Hill. I hoped all would go well.

It transpired that his daughters were attractive young ladies who made the attentive City of London Police very welcome, and there was thus no shortage of volunteers to 'pay attention'. On return, the vicar wrote a glowing letter of appreciation to Snow Hill's Superintendent Terence Howard (respectfully known as 'Wonderloaf'). To use modern jargon, all the wheels had stayed on.

In Petts Wood's Daylight Inn (named after Willett, a Petts Wood resident who first thought of British Summer Time) I met two local retired pressmen with a special interest in St Bride's. I told them of some family City press cuttings and in particular one about their church; they were very interested, and the photographed cutting is now displayed in prime position at the entrance to the crypt, which is open to the public. I quote from the cutting, from which you can read of a prosecution reaching the magistrate before the Crown Prosecution Service, report writing or Legal Aid had been invented.

Thursday, 1 July, 1830 The *Morning Herald*

POLICE
GUILDHALL

Yesterday a decently dressed man, who gave his name as George Gunn, was charged with disturbing the congregation at St Bride's Church on Sunday morning last, by snoring so loudly as to prevent all those who happened to be near him from hearing a single word that was uttered by the Minister.

One of the beadles said that the defendant entered the church, soon after the commencement of the service, in a state of intoxication, and placed himself on a seat that was only calculated to accommodate two persons and was already occupied by that number. He however refused to move and to avoid a disturbance he was left in peaceable possession of the seat; but he had not occupied it two minutes before he fell asleep, and began to snore in the loudest and least harmonious manner possible, so as to distract the attention of all around him from the service that was going on. He made several attempts to rouse him but with very indifferent success, and he was obliged to station himself at his elbow and continue waking him from time to time, in order if possible from seriously annoying the congregation. In this agreeable manner he was occupied for some time but at length the evil reached such a height that he was compelled to remove the defendant and take him to the watch-house.

Sir John Perring said he thought this was hardly a case within his jurisdiction. As the offence was committed in a church, the defendant ought, perhaps, to be handed over to the Ecclesiastical Court.

Here Mr Michael Scales, the Common Councilman, who was waiting in the office, held up his hands in an imploring manner and said, 'Oh, pray don't, Sir John; I can assure you you had much better hang him at once.'

Sir John appeared to be induced by Mr Scales's entreaties not to transfer the defendant to a place where such frightful consequences were to be apprehended and asked Mr Gunn what he had to say in his defence?

Mr Gunn said that neither the education he had received, nor his habits subsequently, had been such as to dispose him to be guilty of any impropriety in a church. He was very much fatigued as he had walked to town from Sydenham that morning; but he denied that he could have been intoxicated as all the liquor he had on the way was one glass of ale which he got at the Edinburgh Castle.

The Alderman considered that one night's imprisonment in the watch-house was a sufficient punishment and the defendant was discharged.

As he was leaving the bar, Mr Scales advised him to be cautious how he went to church for the future.

'Bill Bailey's Night Out'

The Central Criminal Court (the Old Bailey) held a light-hearted informal dinner for court employees, lawyers and police, known as 'Bill Bailey's Night Out', featuring songs, dancing on stage by beautiful athletic-looking young ladies and comedy acts. I invited Peter Jordan of St Batholomew's Hospital (please see the chapter 'Medical Backup'), who after this event suggested a nightcap in St Bartholomew's Hospital Club across the road. I had never been to this club and accompanied Peter with interest.

What happened next was a big surprise, for in the bar was the missing No. 10 police box from West Smithfield. Many years before, when I was Detective Inspector at Snow Hill, the police box was reported missing. All that was left was a hole in the ground, a few wires for telephone and electricity, and the extraordinary loss was never solved. (A collector, scrap-metal dealer or specialist museum was a plausible venue for the heavy iron object.) I looked inside the box, and sure enough it was – No. 10! All we could do was laugh, as the event had long since been forgotten. I was able to get a key to fit the door, which I sent to Peter with a message that within the cupboard would be found a decent first-aid kit, should ever the hospital run short. With the advent of personal radios and mobile telephones, police boxes had since become redundant.

Wood Street Stories

Wood Street police station opened in 1964 and became the new home of 'D' Division for the City of London Police, covering the centre of the City, Barbican, the Bank of England, Mansion House, Guildhall, and later the London Museum. Previously, 'D' Division was based in Cloak Lane police station off Cannon Street, and it was there in 1959 that I was first introduced to City policemen. When Col. Arthur Young arrived in the City from the Metropolitan Police in 1950 (where he had been Assistant Commissioner) he reorganised the Force. Hitherto there had been three 'shifts', known as Early Turn, Late Turn and Night Duty. The new Commissioner, later to be knighted, altered this to a seven-group system, so only one-seventh of the Force was on duty at night, two-sevenths at 7 a.m., one at 8 a.m., another at 9 a.m. and two at 3 p.m. By this deployment, the main strength of the Force was on duty when the City population was at its highest. The Force loved it, and the City was well policed. A side effect of this was that the 'groups' – as they were called – got to know each other very well, bonded, and the team spirit was extraordinary. I was posted to 'A' Group at Cloak Lane, and warmly recall the colleagues with whom I worked. It was a fulfilling, happy experience.

The Wedding of HRH Princess Margaret

An extraordinary day was 6 May 1960, which saw the marriage of HRH Princess Margaret to Anthony Armstrong-Jones. The wedding in Westminster had gone well, and the role of the police in the City of London was later to hold the route for the royal cars to get to Tower Pier near Tower Bridge. The route in the City was from the Embankment, up Queen Victoria Street, across into Cannon Street, then Eastcheap, and finally down to the Tower Pier where HMS *Britannia* awaited to take them on honeymoon.

Richard Dimbleby was commentating for the BBC coverage of this happy event and imminent departure.

Crowds gathered in the City, particularly in Cannon Street, where thousands of office workers, on completion of their nine-to-five day, were heading for trains, each of which would carry well over a thousand passengers. The commuters, wishing to see Princess Margaret, who was late, stayed in Cannon Street to watch, and the numbers continued to swell by hundreds every minute. City Police were out in force, and the line held until two Rolls-Royce cars containing the royal personal suite came through without delay. The crowd, thinking they had missed the royal couple, surged into the street and could not be moved. There was confusion – lateness was the factor. Cannon Street looked like a crowded football club terrace, just a sea of faces, so by the time the honeymooners arrived, the task of getting them to Tower Pier looked impossible. Without diverting, which would have caused even more confusion, the only option was to make a path for the royal car.

We could not regain Cannon Street. The royal car came at last, and the car's bonnet and wings actually pushed the City Police through the crowd. In turn we pushed the crowd out of the way using the power of the car. It was an extraordinary situation; descriptions in the press said that it looked like we were pulling the car through the crowd in a sort of tug of war. We could not stand this pressure for more than thirty yards each, and we had then to drop out to let new fresh colleagues take the strain. Exhausted, we sat on the kerb edge to regain our breath and strength. I had never seen that done before or since. Princess Margaret looked scared in the car – I recall it totally as we struggled to make progress. Shoes, newspapers and debris littered the street, but to my surprise there were no complaints.

At Tower Pier, Richard Dimbleby, now aware of the delay and filling in time, described the history of the Thames, the Tower of London, Tower Bridge, the trees, the shipping over the years, and the ripples of the ebbing tide. The great concern now was that the tide would soon be out and HMS *Britannia* would be unable to leave.

HMS *Britannia* just made it through Tower Bridge and on to

the estuary. Had it grounded, that really would have made news!

Talking to the royal driver on a later occasion, we asked about the car. He told us that over £400 worth of damage, equating currently to about £8,000 when grossed for inflation, was occasioned to the wings and mirrors of the vehicle. He said that at one time he indicated to the detective sitting next to him that the front of the car was lifted off the road and he had no steering. Luckily, the Rolls-Royce had rear-wheel drive.

Car Numbers

Her Majesty The Queen opened the Stock Exchange, Throgmorton Street, in 1972. There was to be the usual line-up of VIPs to be introduced to Her Majesty, including the new City of London Police Commissioner, James Page. Outside we ensured all was going well.

All was well up to the point the presentation line-up was being formed, when it was realised that Prime Minister Edward Heath had not arrived. Word over the radio was that he had left Downing Street in good time and Her Majesty had just left Buckingham Palace. The question was asked, 'Where on earth is he?' Every passing second increased the tension. He could not be late with Her Majesty present – etiquette would not allow it!

In my early days as a constable in Westminster, I had an eye for car numbers. No, I was not like an 'anorak' spotting train numbers, but I, and many other colleagues, found it helpful to know who was about, so we memorised the car numbers of Royalty, senior Government ministers, senior police et cetera. I touched on this in the Introduction.

There was much stress in the Stock Exchange over the absent Prime Minister; this permeated outside and I was asked what could be done. 'He must be somewhere in the City!' said an official in despair. So I took a chance on my memory trivia store to send the following message: 'To all units. Can anyone see Rover motor car, Juliet Uniform Uniform 562?'

A beat officer in Billingsgate Market responded, 'Yes, it's stationary in the market.' A result!

'Get in the car and bring the PM to the Stock Exchange asap,' I said quickly. (The Prime Minister's driver had overshot the

Queen Street turn-off from Upper Thames Street and ended up in Billingsgate Market.)

The Prime Minister arrived at the Stock Exchange about twenty-five seconds before Her Majesty and went straight into the line-up. I hope he was not out of breath, but I bet his blood pressure was raised. Full marks to the beat officer who reacted quickly.

The Stock Exchange removed from Throgmorton Street to Paternoster Square, St Paul's Precinct, in July 2004.

The New London Bridge

On 17 March 1973 HM Queen Elizabeth opened London Bridge. The old London Bridge, sold to the Americans, was dismantled stone by stone and numbered carefully, now standing 'retired' at Lake Havasu City, Arizona, where it was commissioned in October 1971. In London, days before the official bridge opening, an IRA bombing campaign intensified, and in the City we were still reeling from the recent bomb in the Old Bailey. So, for a high-profile event, like the opening of London Bridge, security was intense. For the preceding twenty-four hours, ten pairs of City policemen patrolled the bridge and surrounding streets, and launches of Thames Division, Metropolitan Police, patrolled the river. The Lord Mayor of London, Lord Mais (a civil engineer) was to greet and accompany the Queen; meanwhile, everyone attending the ceremony had to pass through security checks.

During the ceremony, ten bomb-threat calls were received and three calls threatened depth-charge explosions: all were noted and ignored. Her Majesty duly declared the bridge open, but we had to let the huge crowds disperse before traffic was released. It was amazing how everyone left so quickly; many had receptions and lunches to attend, and within half an hour I considered it safe to open the bridge. Inspector John Bull (ex-Grenadier Guards) was on the south side of the bridge and I was on the north side outside the Fishmongers' Hall.* We coordinated the opening by

---

* The Fishmongers' Hall, London Bridge, is the beautiful building of the Fishmongers' Livery Company and has, amongst many treasures, the original 1954 Annigoni portrait of HM The Queen.

radio with Control Centre at Wood Street and the first vehicles released in each direction were *Evening News* vans. So I humbly tell you that, on the day, I actually 'opened' London Bridge! It was yet another memorable occasion.

There was an unexpected sequel. Several times in following weeks we had to shut London Bridge in response to hoax bomb calls (the City was running about forty such calls per day at peak) but they gradually decreased. However, during one exceptional spring tide, when flood alerts had been issued, it looked as though Thames shipping was above the level of the street. We hoped the embankment would hold! A Thames Division patrol crew reported that a strange brown object could now be seen on a buttress under the bridge. All traffic was stopped and a team went into the bridge caverns to access this mystery object. It was a large block of wood left by the constructors and had been there since the bridge was built, unseen when tides were normal... just a bit embarrassing.

Guildhall and St Lawrence Jewry Ceremonial

Annually there is a service in St Lawrence Jewry Church attended by Aldermen, Common Councilmen and Liverymen, all in their official robes, after which they process into Guildhall. Much historic importance is attached to this ancient ceremony and the participants carry flower posies dating back to the time when smells from the City streets required some relief.

The Keeper of the Guildhall, Mr Parker, and his deputy, Mr Marshall, were on duty, one at the rear entrance of the church and the other at Guildhall main door. It was important to signal to the Guildhall Keeper when this procession had commenced, and as I was in uniform I volunteered to give this signal.

This particular year, in the early 1970s, the new Guildhall offices were being constructed and there was a hoarding around the site, leaving a narrow corridor. Some workmen were peering down over the top of this hoarding, each looking like the cartoon character 'Chad' of years ago. I asked them to keep down as they were making the place look untidy. 'If you wish to watch, gentlemen, come out and stand with the crowd – you will then see it all.'

Some came out and others just stood down. The colourful procession was imminent, when a builder, with a wheelbarrow, came through a door in the hoarding. I immediately shouted, 'Come this way, quick!' in an attempt to get the barrow out of the way; that was a mistake. The workman responded instantly and pushed his barrow steadily towards me in the corridor. I guess this was the first time the solemn and historic procession had ever been preceded by a barrow containing wet cement. I cynically pondered that it might become an annual event... perhaps not. It deserved a smile at the time.

The Moorgate Train Crash

I was always very careful to avoid karate matters interfering with police responsibilities, and it was with this in mind that I took one-day annual holiday on Friday, 28 February 1975. I was to travel to Sheffield next day to spend another weekend at a karate event, this time for the Shukokai Karate Union. So I regret I was not on duty at Wood Street when the Northern and City Line train hit the buffers at 8.46 a.m. causing the deaths of forty-three people. However, the incident was well handled by my deputy, Superintendent Don Smith (ex-Captain, Parachute Regiment) and Chief Inspector Brian Fisher. Brian was an expert on major incident planning and procedure – who better to coordinate the police, fire brigade, ambulance and underground railway teams. I heard about the crash on the radio at home and attended later in the day. Next morning I left home early, revisited the scene, then went to Sheffield. On return from Sheffield on the Sunday I again visited the scene. The big problem was heat and lack of air at the site of the crash. Fire brigade teams could only spend fifteen minutes each at the 'sharp end' before becoming exhausted.

I was back at my desk on the Monday when I took a telephone call, as I recall, from an engineering firm at Staines, specialising in air conditioning. They offered a flexible tube fresh-air unit, which they said could be set up in the booking hall, allowing cool air to be pumped direct to the scene. This sounded excellent, so I referred the call, via the police control van at Moorgate Station, to the railway engineers who were in charge. The offer was immediately accepted, fresh air was pumped down the escalator in twelve-inch diameter portable tubes, and rescue teams were much relieved. It was a very sad occasion requiring all hands on deck, including CID, to cope with identification and public enquiries. The inquest was duly held at Guildhall, and subsequent conferences, hosted at Wood Street police station, with medical and interested parties, never conclusively got to the actual reason for the crash; but a lot revolved round the driver of the train, who was also killed.

The Silver Jubilee of HM Queen Elizabeth II

In June 1977 Her Majesty the Queen and the Duke of Edinburgh attended a thanksgiving service at St Paul's Cathedral. St Paul's is in the area of Snow Hill police station, but the boundary runs to the rear of the cathedral, and from there Wood Street police station takes territorial responsibility. After the service there was to be a 'walkabout' along Cheapside to King Street, and from there to the City of London Guildhall, all under Wood Street control. On this day we had support from British Transport, Port of London Authority and Essex Police. The plan was that as the royal party walked along Cheapside, the police lining the route would carefully withdraw ahead at the same pace to foregather at Guildhall, where there would be major crowds and pressure. At the same time we would replace the police lining the route after the royal party had passed by, using a reserve of police positioned near the cathedral. Her Majesty would at no time pass a policeman on her walkabout, thus giving a very good impression of a law-abiding London to national and international television audiences. In Cheapside, an excited male jumped a crush barrier and ran towards Her Majesty, luckily to be stopped by the Commissioner, the last line of defence. I later wrote to Headquarters to suggest that although the overall plan was to give a good impression, it was not ideal for security because the officers lining the route were preoccupied with withdrawing at the same speed as the walkabout, and this was a distraction. Had the police remained static, facing the crowd, any enthusiastic hurdler – or worse – could be seen earlier and stopped in the act.

Apart from the 1977 November Lord Mayor's Show, this was my last major 'ceremonial' in the Force, and I was pleased to have been in at the 1953 Coronation in Westminster and now at the Jubilee in the City. All thoughts about karate were put aside on this day! All had gone well on Wood Street's area.

Just before the royal party came from the precincts of the cathedral to walk along Cheapside, I caught site of a St Bartholomew's Hospital patient in a wheelchair being pushed by two staff wearing the Bart's Hospital shield on their coats. The crowd was packed six deep, and the patient, three rows back, stood no chance of seeing anything. I previously had just got a wheelchair-bound person through to the front by unhooking the metal barriers, but in any crowd, however good-humoured, there are selfish people who will take advantage and dislodge some others who have been patiently waiting at the front. It was too late. Her Majesty's walkabout was imminent, and in spite of the special relationship between the City Police and St Bartholomew's Hospital I could not arrange it in time. This was a very small incident, but the image has remained with me. It would have meant a lot to the wheelchair patient and with hindsight I regret I did not act faster. Otherwise, I enjoyed the busy day.

Assistance to Metropolitan Police at New Cross

On Saturday, 13 August 1977, there was a march and demonstration at New Cross in the Metropolitan Police area, at which the City of London Police assisted. There was always good cooperation between the two forces when possible problems were anticipated, and on this occasion a confrontation was anticipated between the Socialist Workers' Party and the National Front, complicated by Millwall football supporters being due to exit their home ground nearby. Deputy Assistant Commissioner David Helm of the Metropolitan Police was in charge with a very large Metropolitan Police reserve, and I was responsible for the City Police contingent of one hundred. It was an afternoon of action. Overall there were 214 arrests and 110 casualties, fifty-six of which were police. It was the first occasion when riot shields were used by Metropolitan Police on the streets of London, and rioting erupted along the route to Lewisham. For several weeks I was very conscious of anything moving in the air, such as birds, for we had become very wary of missiles on that Saturday afternoon. This day will always be remembered in contrast with the many memorable peaceful public occasions and happier times. No time to think of karate that weekend, either!

St Stephen's Church, Walbrook

A difficult situation occurred in 1977 when the City Police, acting on excellent information, surrounded St Stephen's Church, Walbrook, home of the Samaritans since their foundation in 1953. The objective was to prevent the escape and facilitate the arrest of a man wanted on warrant for armed robbery, who had entered the church to take refuge.

The duty officer at the scene telephoned to declare that the Reverend Dr Chad Varah, founder of the Samaritans, was complaining about the police presence, which he regarded as an unwelcome pressure, and was refusing to allow police to enter his church.

The Samaritans are a highly respected organisation, with Royal Family and City support. The Prince of Wales is patron.

(I was later interested to know that Dr Varah, a graduate of Keble College, Oxford, was one of the writers behind the 'Dan Dare' space cartoon series.)

I was wary that the City of London Police would receive adverse publicity if we acted in a heavy-handed manner, but here was a situation where a court of law had issued an arrest warrant, and the arrest would have to be the end result. I attended the church in uniform, where I met Dr Chad Varah in his vestry. He told me that he felt oppressed by the heavy police presence in Walbrook, and that in the history of the Samaritans, police had never entered a church to make an arrest. He regarded a church as a sanctuary and was concerned that the public should continue to feel able to take refuge and get advice within without being arrested.

I told him that in this case an arrest warrant had been issued by a court of law, which required that the person named should be arrested and brought before the court: that must be the outcome. However, I was prepared to respect his wish to scale down the police presence on condition that, after church interviewing was complete, the suspect should be handed over to police in Walbrook. This was agreed. We shook hands and I then reduced the police presence to two constables, who would stand across the road waiting to be called to make the arrest. Dr Chad Varah accompanied me to the door, and I considered this to be a reasonable agreement and outcome. I went back to my desk at Wood Street.

What happened next caused me much embarrassment. Dr Varah came to the church door about half an hour later, saw the policemen waiting across the road, looked around, then went back inside the church. Next, the 'accused', running fast, exited and went north in Walbrook, escaping into the Bank underground station. There was no apology from the church, and the founder of the Samaritans refused to be seen. It was obvious to us, but unprovable, that there had been a conspiracy to pervert the wishes of the court. The police lived to fight another day, but the credibility of Dr Chad Varah and the Samaritans, under discussion in Wood Street canteen, was much damaged; nor did I escape due criticism.

Mystery Bank Raid – Lloyds Baker Street

During a weekend in September 1971, I was the Duty Chief Superintendent for the City when from the Metropolitan Police came a message that there was an urgent need to trace a bank which was 'under attack'. The bank had three local characteristics: it was near traffic lights, near a restaurant and near roadworks. A radio ham had intercepted communications being used by a rooftop criminal looking out to advise his in-bank conspirators. In the overheard two-way conversations, the lookout referred to roadworks and traffic lights. At one time it was said that a waiter from a nearby restaurant had tried to look through the window of the bank.

The City houses a mass of banks, national and international, and it was incumbent on us to make absolutely sure that the attack was not taking place in the 'square mile'. The duty Detective Chief Inspector was Gerald Squires (who later became Detective Chief Superintendent in charge of the City Fraud Department). He and I drove in our private cars to the City –

traffic being quiet on a Sunday – to urgently rendezvous and discuss how we could deal with this pressing problem. The three City divisions were alerted, and the traffic branch was consulted about known roadworks. We all scoured the City looking for banks linked to the specified criteria, coming to the conclusion that the ongoing bank raid was not in the City, and commiserating with the Metropolitan Police on their huge task of trying to trace the venue.

On Monday morning, next day, we were still anxious to know the venue of the criminal activity and sensed the stakes were very high. News then broke that it was Lloyds Bank at Baker Street, outside the City. Gerry Squires and I were relieved, but knew our Metropolitan colleagues were going to have a difficult time.

I now read, thirty-seven years later, that a film is being made about this bank raid, which includes the security services, allegations of corruption and hints of D notices for the press. Who would have thought that this 1971 event would re-erupt in 2008?

Lloyd's of London

When at City Police Headquarters, 26 Old Jewry (which links Cheapside to Gresham Street), I was able to enjoy reasonably stable hours and often catch the same train each day from Cannon Street direct to Petts Wood, Kent, my local station. I got used to seeing fellow commuters and soon engaged in regular conversations during the journey. David Penning, an architect; Geoffrey Gass, a building society secretary (who later became chairman of the City of London Police Committee); Gordon Muir, an accountant; Chris Howland, Cambridge and Kent cricketer, an investment advisor; Ben Sullivan, Bank of England official and toastmaster; Ron Miller, an assistant director of Holmwoods, Back and Manson, Lloyd's Underwriters; Henry Martin, solicitor, of Stafford Clark and Co.; Ronald Blake, Manager of Cazenove Stockbrokers; and my brother, Robin, of City Police CID, formed the core of the discussions. A centre of attraction was a vivacious young manageress who ran a dress shop in Bishopsgate and got out at Chislehurst before reaching Petts Wood. We formed a club and acquired a tie with the City shield and '1803' emblazoned thereon. Some thought it was a historic City club, but in fact it was the time of the train out of Cannon Street!

Through this contact a memorable, happy association evolved between the City Police and Lloyd's of London. Ron Miller suggested a walking competition on a Saturday afternoon. As a result, teams from Metropolitan Police, City Police, City Police Cadets, Lloyd's, St Dunstan's Home for the Blind and the Royal Greenjackets competed on a 'twice round the City' route: it was initially won by Lloyd's, who had some star athletes, including Olympic walker, Olly Flynn. The Metropolitan Police Walking Club members ably assisted the blind St Dunstan's competitors by being connected with a cord, and only good, experienced walkers could do this, as St Dunstan's had a very good team. The results, recording and organisation initially fell to the City Police Athletic Club (of which I was Chairman), but as the biennial event got bigger it outgrew Wood Street police station and moved to a nearby large restaurant at Barrington House, run by manager Peter Nowak of Mecca Leisure. Lloyd's firms hired rooms for the afternoon, Mecca organised the catering and there was dancing to a band whilst the results were calculated by a team of Lloyd's accountants – and in the final years by computers. It became a major event, needing policing along the route through London Wall, Smithfield, Farringdon Street and Ludgate Hill, but there was never an untoward incident.

Lloyd's of London insured the event and encouraged their brokers and underwriters to participate in large numbers. All the proceeds, entry fees and sponsorships went to Lloyd's of London British Legion, who looked after welfare at military hospitals, including Woolwich, Germany, Belfast, the Falklands and anywhere where there was a British military presence. As a result of this, the grateful military responded by joining the walks and at one time we had over a thousand participating. Large sums of money were raised for this cause and it was put to excellent use.

A driving force character from Lloyd's was Andrew Drysdale, who had a strong senior military background. On the day of the race he dressed in top hat and tails, and harangued and encouraged the participants through a loudhailer. Finally he stood on the steps of Wood Street police station to use a starting pistol handed to him by Sergeant Tony Armfield, Secretary of the City of London Police Athletic Club. (The pistol was quickly returned to the safe!)

Annually at Lloyd's of London, there was a dinner and cabaret for disabled ex-servicemen – several hundred attending. The Star and Garter Home, St Dunstan's, Chelsea Royal Hospital, the Guinea Pig Club and others were represented. Ron Miller organised this event, which was attended by the Chairman of Lloyd's and matrons from the military hospitals. There were some very emotional moments when seriously injured, but recovering, servicemen spoke to show their appreciation, including Simon Weston of the Welsh Guards, who was badly burned in the Falklands War.

There needed to be cooperation and organisation to get these special guests to Lloyd's and into the Captain's Cabin, where the event took place. To assist, many ex-service City Police, including some younger members of the Force, volunteered to attend in their own time in uniform to assist with the ambulances and logistics of parking in the area of Lime Street. Sergeants Eric Thornborrow and John Rew, ably assisted by WPC Belinda Harding, were stalwarts in this operation. The evening was a combined operation willingly given to show respect and appreciation for our armed forces. Lloyd's catering and waitress staff all volunteered to give their services free.

On one occasion the military ambulance, carrying a lot of army personnel after the Lloyd's event, broke down in the City and was declared irreparable. Chief Superintendent Bob Fowlie (ex-Royal Navy, HMS *Belfast*) opened up Bishopsgate police station, including the bar, and the party continued until alternative arrangements were made in the early hours. It was thereafter talked about annually in glowing terms.

Members of the City Police who had helped were invited to witness the two minutes' silence on Armistice Day. It was eerie and very impressive: members on the floor of Lloyd's stood at their desks, the telephones stopped and the Lutine Bell* was rung

---

* The famous Lutine Bell is normally rung when an important announcement is to be made from the Rostrum. It is rung twice before good news and once before bad news. An occasion when the bell was rung for news not connected with shipping

to signal the start and conclusion of this annual act of respect and remembrance. Utter silence prevailed.

Several ex-service members of the City of London Police had medical operations in the Queen Elizabeth Royal Military Hospital at Woolwich and were soon back on duty.

Alas, Ron Miller died after an illness, having worked fifty years at Lloyd's where he was a household name. He had received the MBE from HM The Queen for coordinating Lloyd's services to the military hospitals, and was accorded a funeral with full military honours at Woolwich, where the Chief Surgeon, a Brigadier, gave the eulogy and the Lloyd's of London Choir sang. Members of the City of London Police also attended. It was an appreciative response for the help and support Ron Miller and Lloyd's had provided over the years and before the reins were taken over by others. A senior officer of the Royal Army Medical Corps related to me that they were considering placing a brass plaque in the bar of the hospital, reading 'Ron Miller used to sit here', to perpetuate his memory, but before this came about there were cutbacks and the Military Hospital was closed, to be taken over by the local National Health Service.

Operation Fullemploy

Long after the air-raid death of my mother in 1940, my father married into another City of London Police family by marrying Jane Geeves, a widow, whose late husband, also a City of London policeman, had seen wartime naval action against the *Graf Spee* in the legendary Battle of the River Plate. Jane was the sister of City of London Police Superintendent John Vennard. So I knew Linda, a young relation of the Vennards, who rang me at Wood Street, asking for some advice and help.

Linda was a lovely secretary employed locally by Barclays Bank International, and her telephone call was a surprise. She was heavily involved in a project called 'Operation Fullemploy', the admirable objective of which was to advise and encourage those

was at the announcement of the death of HM King George VI in 1952. From 1799 to 1859 the Lutine Bell lay on the seabed, for it was the bell of HMS *Lutine*, sunk in a gale off the Dutch coast. It was originally a French ship captured by the British. (Source: *Britannica*) who were having difficulty in gaining employment. The advice and instruction extended to pupils was on typing and office skills, personal appearance and presentation, production of typed curriculum vitae and so on.

Linda explained that there was an 'anti-police' undertone among the thirty pupils, mainly due to the local environment where they lived in inner London, such as Brixton. It was suggested that it would be helpful to the bank and the course if someone could explain to the pupils the way the police service was financed and what would ideally be a good police/public relationship. I felt there could be scope for a whole course on that subject alone!

So I offered to help Linda by attending the course, speaking to the pupils for one hour, with the second hour for questions. The first hour went well, but when the second session commenced I came in for some hostile questioning, mainly from the males, which caused me to realise that there was a huge rift and strong feeling in the Metropolitan Police area. After the session, the Barclays Bank people were concerned and apologetic about the pressure of the questioning so I reassured them that I was not the slightest bit offended: it was the police in general who were being criticised here and there was nothing personal. I tried my best to give the police side of the situation but was disappointed at the strength of the pupils' feelings. A lot of talking would be necessary to bring sides together – a huge long-term project for others. It was not sorted until after the Brixton riots.

One young lady asked, 'A friend of mine owes money to a mail order catalogue and is worried about any knock at the door. She can now pay but is frightened to contact them in case she is arrested at her new address. What should she do?'

I responded that I did not wish to give open advice on that specific problem because I did not know all the details, but said I would leave my telephone number with Barclays Bank. If the person concerned wished to contact me I would confidentially help as much as possible.

What happened next I did not expect. Two attractive young ladies from the course called at Wood Street. I think the station officers wondered what I was up to – they would never have guessed! Both had catalogue debts and wished to clear them, if possible avoiding legal action or prosecution. I considered the situation, and taking the broadest view told myself there could be no harm in helping them. Obviously the Operation Fullemploy course had made them realise that they must start with a clean, open sheet – 'no skeletons in the cupboard' – and here was their response: to clear their debts, a very good start indeed. I telephoned the respective catalogue houses, asked to speak to the security officers, declared who I was and my involvement, and asked for details of the debts.

Having established the details, I arranged for the girls to get money orders at London Wall post office and we posted off the debts, having been told that all recovery action would be withdrawn on receipt of the money. The girls were delighted and obviously told their colleagues. It did not end there; two more pairs of girls called and similar debts were cleared! This activity did not appear in any police instruction book but the overall result was a good one and I hope the girls got regular employment without any more deception.

I heard that Barclays Bank was pleased.

The Miss World Organisation and Karate Security

In 1969, when trouble flared on the streets of Belfast and some other towns in Northern Ireland, the Commissioner of Police for the City of London, Sir Arthur Young, was seconded to Northern Ireland by James Callaghan, MP, Home Secretary, to bring about recommended reforms. During his distinguished career in the City of London, Sir Arthur had been seconded to the Gold Coast, Kenya and Malaya at times of trouble. Northern Ireland was going to be difficult.

James Page, appointed Acting Commissioner in Sir Arthur's absence, looked at the City Police recruiting figures and expressed concern. Surrounded by the Metropolitan Police, with a large public relations department, he felt that the City of London Police needed a higher profile. If the City Police could attract publicity – and we had a lot to offer – then increased public awareness would have a beneficial effect on recruiting. The Acting Commissioner introduced the red-and-white-check cap-bands, City of London colours. This had good effect, for it gave higher visibility on the streets, and television shots of the Force, for example, outside the Central Criminal Court, accentuated the differences between the City and Metropolitan Police.

So there was official enthusiasm to seek publicity for the City Police, and I was asked to give thought to implementing this policy. The first event was an exhibition at the Royal Exchange to be opened by the Lord Mayor. A stream of visitors included HM Chief Inspector of Constabulary and at lunchtimes the exhibition was very crowded and popular. A huge banner on the Royal Exchange advertised the event across the Bank junction, and we could not have had a better site.

Next, exclusively for the *Daily Telegraph*, there was a combined picture of the Force assembled in Barbican. The divisions, headquarters departments, cars, motorbikes, cadets, canoes, dogs and horses were all involved, the plan being to publish the picture on half a page (which was valuable in public relations terms), with the other half-page being an explanation of who was in the picture. It was duly published, but production was nearly a disaster. When the *Daily Telegraph* photographer, Robert Hope, was ready, the heavens opened to snow and rain and the light dropped dramatically! We all took cover, hastily reassembling before an even blacker cloud loomed. The picture was duly taken, and the wet state of all did not show; nor was the rushed assembly too evident. We were lucky to get the published picture.

In November 1969 I was writing at home when my wife called, 'Come and see the last six Miss Worlds live.' We sat and watched, together with 18 million other television viewers: it was the BBC's biggest audience, huge in TV terms. It occurred to me that if we invited next year's 1970 contestants to the City, it would attract a lot of publicity. I spoke to the Acting Commissioner, contacted the Miss World office and met the organiser, Julia Morley. The contestants came to the City, visiting Whitbread's shire horses and the City Police horses. They went to Lloyd's of London, momentarily stopping all business on the trading floor, concluding with a visit to Wood Street police station, then lunch at nearby Barrington House, hosted by Mecca, which Eric Morley and the Acting Commissioner attended. The publicity was immense; nearly every daily and Sunday paper carried pictures, and front page pictures are valuable. Whitbread's horses, Lloyd's of London, City of London Police and contestants' pictures went round the world.

The following year the contestants visited St Paul's Cathedral, the Tower of London and Wood Street again, this time on a Saturday. They also took part in the Lord Mayor's show.

Eric and Julia Morley were pleased with these visits and publicity, but they had security problems and telephoned for advice. First, a group called the 'Angry Brigade' had set off a bomb at the rear of the Royal Albert Hall in the Metropolitan Police area on the eve of live broadcasting, causing security to be doubled. Julia Morley asked about help from off-duty policemen, but this was out of the question. I explained that one of the karate groups in the British Karate Control Commission, as part of their discipline, always dressed smartly in grey flannels and blazers, with white shirt and association tie. That night, thirty British Karate Kyokushinkai (BKK) karateka reported to the Royal Albert Hall, manning fire exits and making themselves generally helpful. Mecca settled with the BKK direct. I kept my fingers crossed and the karateka gave a very good impression: they were fit and keen, responding promptly and willingly at short notice.

There was also trouble with Women's Liberation and Animal Rights groups (fur coats being an issue). The Miss World event was very high profile, and demonstrators tried to capitalise on this chance of publicity. Julia Morley rang again, asking if I knew of a linguist with secretarial ability who could run part of the Miss World office specialising in chaperones and sponsors. I did. I telephoned Jennifer Rutland, my multilingual cousin, who was employed by Southern Television in Brighton. She took a holiday and moved into the Waldorf Hotel for two weeks; they could not have had a better person – Jennifer, a graduate with film and television experience, was the ideal person.

Julia Morley then telephoned (she spoke very fast and I had to listen carefully) asking if I knew of any Japanese-speaking young lady who could look after Miss Japan and Miss Korea. Through karate, I knew a charming young lady called Tami, employed as a singer in a London club. I telephoned her. She also took leave, with permission of her employers, though I had to visit her manager to ensure approval. She duly moved in to the Waldorf Hotel, and her contribution was exceptional as she knew a large number of contacts in London. On the night of the Miss World contest, for example, Miss Japan walked the catwalk with such valuable gems round her neck that only the jeweller in attendance was allowed to fix and unfix the necklace. Miss Yugoslavia, who had arrived under-equipped, wore dresses supplied by Tami. On the night of relaxation, when all contestants at a Mecca restaurant in the City performed and provided their own entertainment, Tami sang the hit songs 'Feelings' and 'San Francisco' with such skill that she received a standing ovation.

One other telephone call deserves mention: it was said that contestants had indicated in a questionnaire their wish to meet young policemen in London. Could I arrange sixty-three young policemen to come to a private disco and buffet at Silks in Tottenham Court Road? This nearly caused me to fuse! I could foresee all sorts of problems, but on the positive side here was potential for a great night out which, like that in *Cinderella*, would have to come to an end at midnight. I advised Julia Morley that the 'sixty-three young policemen proposition' was impossible, but I would have a notice put up in the single men's quarters for thirty-one off-duty policemen. The list was quickly filled. I rang the Commanding Officer of the Royal Naval Air Station at Yeovilton, whom I had recently met when HM The Queen opened the London Museum at London Wall. He duly arranged a competition, as a result of which thirty-two Fleet Air Arm pilots also attended. A good time was had by all, and the ex-police I now meet in retirement still talk about it!

At the conclusion, Mecca-hired coaches arrived for the police and Fleet Air Arm pilots, who were duly collected, the police just for the short journey back to the City. I was puzzled by the coach driver. I knew I had seen him before but could not remember where. As we alighted at Wood Street after midnight, I thanked him and asked where we had met before. 'I used to cut your hair on Saturday mornings,' he responded. It all came back to me in a rush. I attended a barber's shop in Orpington, and one Saturday he was not there. I enquired after him, and the proprietor informed me that he had been wanted for safe-blowing all over Essex and was now detained in secure premises! Several years had elapsed...

Malicious bomb alerts were a problem. In the Britannia Hotel in the early hours of the night, the contestants, chaperones, management and sponsors were roused from their beds and ushered into the corridors. Eric Morley rang, asking if could I meet the Mecca management in the hotel, to advise on what they should do, as it was disrupting sleep and causing irritation to all. The contestants in particular understandably did not wish to be seen in their overnight attire and face packs. This situation was a great shame, for the Miss World Organisation and Mecca raised huge sums of money for children's charities through the Variety Club of Great Britain and they did not deserve this aggravation. Elsewhere in London the Irish Republican Army (IRA) activity and consequent bomb scares were causing disruption to business and travel.

The City of London Police had published a policy document about bomb scares, with a film about the handling of bomb alerts, which we showed to City business houses, bankers, shippers, insurance office staff et cetera. I had a word with the Commissioner, as this Mecca request was to take me into the Metropolitan Police area. He approved that I should go, as it was not a public arrangement. So I went to the Britannia Hotel, spoke to the assembled Mecca management – about thirty people – and recommended a policy based on our City Police advice. The false bomb alerts stopped immediately. The culprits must have been 'close' to the hotel, a situation we had experienced before. Sometimes the problem can be originated by a person near to the scene, and if they know the effect is being minimised the hoax calls will cease.

Mary and I were subsequently invited to the Royal Albert Hall to watch the live television broadcast, and then to the Café de Paris for the celebration dinner and dance. On arrival we looked at the seating plan and found to our surprise that we were sitting at the newly crowned Miss World's table with Mr and Mrs Morley and several titled couples. My wife asked me, 'What have we done to deserve this?' Whatever had been done was obviously appreciated, though I would have been very pleased and grateful for a lower profile. It was a memorable and interesting night.

I repeated the talk the next year in advance of the event. Security was also supplemented with some new karate players, all smart, fit and dressed in blazers and grey flannels et cetera. For several years I assisted, with the Commissioner's approval, and was ably supported by the Mecca management and the karateka. When I eventually went to work for Mecca (mentioned later in this chapter), I again addressed the Mecca management in the Waldorf Hotel, this time as 'one of them'. I stressed the need to be alert and keep fit. We also had CCTV coverage in the corridors on the first floor, monitored twenty-four hours. Some of the contestants were political security risks: Miss Israel, Miss South Africa and Miss Cyprus, for example. One evening we split into smaller groups to visit restaurants, and I went to a Piccadilly restaurant where I chose duck. It was undercooked and I felt very ill next day, being repeatedly sick. However, having emphasised the need for 'security' to keep fit and alert, I could not admit to being unwell and did not enjoy the will power needed to keep going. The family kept me supplied with clean clothing, but at the end of the two weeks I went home very tired and relieved! During those two weeks we had, amongst other engagements, visited the Houses of Parliament for lunch, the City, Jersey for a charity event, Beaulieu Motor Museum, Woburn Safari Park, the show *Evita* and the *Cutty Sark* via the Thames. At Jersey, in the Channel Islands, I arranged for all-night Securicor patrols in the hotel grounds, and we had chartered an aeroplane for the return trip.

Invited to lunch by Julia Morley, I duly met her at the Sportsman in Tottenham Court Road. I discussed my involvement with the BKCC and asked if she thought the Mecca Organisation might sponsor some karate events. A meeting was arranged with Eric Morley, the Chairman and Chief Executive, and one Saturday morning at eight o'clock we met at Mecca House, Southwark. I was expected at the door, which was re-secured after I entered: security was good. Bryn Williams and I subsequently met Don McCallion, a development director, and architect's plans were drawn for a major high-street bowling club to be totally converted to martial arts with purpose-built administration offices and training areas for fitness, judo, karate, kendo et cetera. It would have been revolutionary and a 'first' in this country. The project was discussed within the BKCC, and here some old animosity resurrected, such as who would benefit? Which groups would use it? Would it be fair on local clubs to have this venue opened? I was very disappointed to encounter this negative stance, so we let the project drift, and Mecca didn't press us for progress. However, some BKCC organisations ran weekend courses and competitions in Mecca branches. A very successful event, for example, was staged by Steve Arneil with the BKK in the Birmingham Tower Ballroom, Edgbaston, where they had a large adjacent lakeside car park for coaches and cars.

Linda Applegate, Eric Morley's personal assistant, telephoned.

Mr Morley was abroad and unable to use two VIP tickets for the London premier of the Muhammad Ali film *The Greatest* at the Empire, Leicester Square. Could I deputise for him with a guest? Yes, please! Jim Elkin of the British Aikido Association and I duly attended, dinner-jacketed, saw the film in prime seats, and then adjourned to the Sportsman at Tottenham Court Road, where a reception was prepared. It was a great evening. I asked Muhammad Ali to sign the VIP ticket, along with Henry Cooper and Terry Downes, triple boxing champions sitting together. Later this ticket was auctioned at a City Police charity boxing event, raising £200.

Eric Morley had already arranged for me to be an honorary member of the Sportsman Club. Sport liaison was through Derek Ufton, ex-Charlton and England centre half and an accomplished cricketer, who was very helpful. I subsequently met many karate leaders at the Sportsman, including Tatsuo Suzuki and Keinsoke Eneoda, plus referees from abroad. I also attended special 'Sportsman Personality of the Month' awards compèred by Jimmy Hill. It was an oasis, where one could meet quietly in first-class surroundings.

On one occasion in January 1973 I caused consternation to the management, which could also have given me much personal trouble. When signing in at the reception desk with a South African guest, I accidentally dropped my police warrant card. Though I was checked in with my Sportsman card, the staff had no idea I was in the police service and I could not understand the 'buzz' of staff looking round the lounge door to see what I was doing. I was simply drinking tea and talking to Hugh Thomson, karate referee, who had just arrived in London and was due to referee the Fanfare for Europe match – Great Britain against France at Crystal Palace on 13 January. My warrant card was returned at reception. I thanked the staff – leaving a suitable gratuity – and apologised. Losing a warrant card is the equivalent of losing a rifle in the military. They had wondered if I had been on police observation, but answered their own concerns as time progressed.

In 1977, Julia Morley said the Mecca Organisation was looking for a Head of Security and asked if I might be interested. I had worked nearly eight years at Wood Street (and over seven years with the BKCC) and had been impressed by the Mecca staff. I liked their style; it was energetic and different. As a youngster I had played a lot of Monopoly at home and knew that if one had the opportunity to get Trafalgar Square or Coventry Street, then one should go for it: there would be one chance only! With this example in mind, I thought it over, discussed it at home and, though I had been very happy and lucky in the City, decided to join Mecca: another challenge and another story. I subsequently spent thirteen memorable years with Mecca, which went by very quickly. Biennially, there is now a Mecca reunion, when one can renew acquaintances with former colleagues. They were dedicated, special people. I learned a lot from them, after which I knew that had I the opportunity to go back to Wood Street, I would have been much better equipped with the extra knowledge; that was fanciful thinking, but the truth.

I reflect that if Mary, my wife, had not called on me to watch the 'last six' back in 1969, none of this karate-related Mecca activity would have happened.

Pleasant Surprises

A Surprise in the Post

In the early 1970s there was much publicity about corruption in Hong Kong, and press speculation that an anti-corruption team would be sent there came to fruition. This became known as the ICAC – the Independent Commission Against Corruption.

My views on corruption were reasonably well known amongst police colleagues. There had been several high-profile prosecutions, and when the subject was raised in general discussion I usually had a comment to contribute.

At home I was reading the morning newspaper about Hong Kong corruption when I heard the post drop on the doormat. There was a letter in a '10 Downing Street' envelope (I recognised the printing style from my days working on duty in No. 10). Oh my goodness, I thought, are they going to send me to Hong Kong? Why No. 10 and not the Home Office? With hindsight, all this was very presumptuous.

I sat down, wary of what I was about to read. The letter informed me that it was in mind to recommend to Her Majesty the Queen that I be appointed as an Ordinary Officer of the Civil Division of the Most Excellent Order of the British Empire (OBE). I responded by hand, carefully reading my reply several times before posting it, as I had written in a state of surprise, shock and excitement. I duly attended Buckingham Palace with my wife and two eldest children on 15 June 1974 – a memorable day, when I met Her Majesty.

At this time Irish Republican Army bombing activity was keeping police very busy in London, and I had read press reports that in the Midlands a minister of religion had passed some addresses of senior police officers to IRA suspects. I kept a low profile about the investiture, with no photographs, which I now regret. I took one-day annual holiday from work, and after the investiture we drove to the Tower Hotel, next to Tower Bridge, for lunch, where we were well looked after by the chief security officer, Richard Johnston, and the hotel manager. Both had been so helpful with the recent European Karate Union Congress, and I knew there would be a welcome.

At the New Tokyo Restaurant, then in Swallow Street off Piccadilly, Mary and I celebrated with Sir Walter and Lady Winterbottom, Director of the Sports Council, the Commissioner of Police for the City of London, James Page and Shirley Page, and Bryn and Mary Williams, BKCC General Secretary. We had a good evening and all had been very supportive.

A Surprise Visit

A memorable figurehead in Japan was Ryoichi Sasakawa, multi-millionaire and charity benefactor whose profile listed no less than thirty-seven interests, ranging from the Japan Shipbuilding Industry Foundation, Japan Civil Aviation Promotion Foundation to traditional arts, the World Union of Karate-do Organisations and Kendo. During the Second World War he had donated several airfields to the Japan war effort and at the conclusion of the war it was determined that he should serve three years' imprisonment. On 12 December 1945, he presented himself at Sugamo Prison, marching at the head of three brass bands, of which he was sponsor and president: some style! With Japan Olympic connections, Ryoichi Sasakawa visited Great Britain to meet the Duke of Edinburgh at Buckingham Palace, the Minister for Sport, Eldon Griffiths, and later the Lord Mayor of London, Sir Robin Gillett, at the Mansion House. On 26 July he also paid his second visit to Wood Street police station where, as president of FAJKO and WUKO, he presented me with a certificate of an Honorary 7th Dan, Karate, from the Federation of All-Japan Karate-do Organisations. His first visit to Wood Street was on 17 February 1976, when he attended a dinner hosted by the BKCC. It was a memorable evening, during which Mrs Sasakawa played the *biwa*, a traditional Japanese musical instrument, and Major John Green (UKKF), Deputy Chairman BKCC, made a suitable presentation to commemorate the Sasakawa visit. Julia Morley of Mecca Ltd., Derek Langham (KUGB and also Deputy Chairman of BKCC) and senior officers of the Force attended.

A Surprise Event

Also in 1977 at Wood Street, I received a call from the British Kendo Association. They had a dilemma which they hoped could be resolved. The Japanese World Kendo team and supporters, stopping overnight in London en route from the United States of America to Japan, wished to practise with the British Kendo Association. There was difficulty in finding a suitably floored venue in central London, carpeting being unsuitable. Kendo is the 'aristocrat' of martial arts and I knew that the party of about twenty would be a group of very senior professors and emeritus professors from Japan universities, themselves senior in kendo – in fact the pinnacle of world kendo. At Wood Street we were blessed with a large hall and a top-quality floor of South African wood, afromosia, which I knew would be ideal. Luckily the request was for a Friday evening, so I telephoned the Commissioner, who had no objection. I also learned that he and the Assistant Commissioner, who lived in flats above Wood Street police station, would be away for the weekend; that was helpful news because kendo is a very noisy activity.

The British Kendo Association and the Japanese World Kendo group faced each other to enjoy a superb and noisy evening, during which I hoped the passing public would not think we were interviewing prisoners! The floor was pronounced excellent and all were very pleased.

Afterwards, during refreshments, there was a visiting card 'ritual' when many visiting cards were exchanged, and on rereading these later I realised that Wood Street and the British Kendo Association had hosted a really memorable event. It was probably the most unusual sports event ever to have taken place in a police station.

Surprises in Retirement

I retired in March 1991 after thirteen happy years at Mecca working for Michael Guthrie, Chairman, and the Managing

Directors, Michael Woods and Barry Anderson. Team spirit and enthusiasm at head office had been a pleasure to experience. There was a happy crew. The Rank Organisation was to take over the company, and the Mecca board stood down as anticipated changes came about. One of the changes was that Mecca head office in Southwark would close, and the computers and staff transferred to Rank premises. I was asked by Rank to oversee these changes. Having already written to Michael Guthrie indicating my wish to retire on 31 March 1991, the next few months were going to be sad, as furniture and company culture were shifted. Rank offered me a bonus of £2,000 for managing a trouble-free transition – I would have done it for nothing, but accepted their offer. The last day in Mecca head office brought about tears for many. Some in similar circumstances would be forgiven for wishing to cease work early on the last day, then adjourn to a local hostelry for farewell drinks, but this last day was crazily busy. I arrived at 7 a.m., and by 6 p.m. just had to walk away from what was left. I could not do any more, declaring my innings closed and leaving the overnight security company in charge.

On my first day of retirement, while 'at ease' at home, Ben Sullivan, ex-Bank of England Official, toastmaster to the Lord Mayor of London and member of the '1803 Club' (referred to in 'Wood Street Stories – Lloyd's of London'), called at my house to present a litter stick and welcome me to PALs (Pensioners Against Litter), a local group of volunteers who clear litter discarded by uncaring members of the public, motorists and in particular smokers.

Now retired, Ben Sullivan is a remarkable man. When twenty-four years old he was commissioned in the Royal Navy, having volunteered for special wartime operations. He helped deliver the 1st Battalions of the Hampshire and Dorset Regiments to Gold Beach, Arromanche on D-Day, 4 June 1944, the first sea landings of British troops on that historic day. As toastmaster, he had officiated at twenty-seven Lord Mayors' Banquets in Guildhall, and 250 State functions in the City. Many times I had driven Ben to his home late at night after City functions and he had reciprocated by driving me home when I had been on duty. On his eightieth birthday, the Corporation of London gave a

Guildhall banquet in his honour, attended by over one hundred guests including five ex-Lord Mayors and Eddie George, Governor of the Bank of England.

With the new litter stick I commenced 'picking' for PALs, arising early on Sundays, when the absence of parked cars allowed access, to clear litter – and later, graffiti. The graffiti problem increased, needing a lot of attention, and we were well supported by Bromley Council and the local Residents' Association.

In 2006 the telephone rang and a female voice announced, 'This is the Home Office. I am very pleased to inform you that you have won a Respect award of £1,000 for "Taking a Stand".' I was very wary, owing to a 1961 telephone call, which I will now describe.

My daughter Caroline was born at home in May 1961, and I had arranged fourteen days' summer holiday in order to help look after my wife and the new baby. I let it be known amongst colleague sergeants at Snow Hill that I was also going to realign a garden path and build a brick wall in the front garden. Leaning on a spade, contemplating the project, I was distracted by the telephone.

Woman's voice: 'Mr Francis?' (I confirmed.) 'This is Bromley Council. Will you hold the line, please? The Borough Surveyor wishes to speak to you.' I duly held the line, wondering what was going to happen next.

Man's voice: 'Mr Francis, thank you for holding. I am the Deputy Borough Surveyor. The Borough Surveyor has asked me to phone you regarding a report that you have taken delivery of bricks and sand but we cannot trace a planning application. Would you mind telling me what you are planning to do?'

I explained what I was planning to do, making it sound as simple as possible.

'Have you allowed for drainage?' asked the 'Surveyor', alias Sergeant Peter Rowe. Oh, damn, I thought. I cannot tell him that I intend to leave a gap in the bricks! He continued, 'I'm sorry, but you will have to suspend work for the time being and I will transfer you to the forms department.'

Forms Department? That didn't sound right and I challenged it. Forms Department, alias Sergeant Tibbenham, came on the line. The two of them, plus the policewoman, had me 'wobbling' for longer than I care to admit.

Now, reverting to the Home Office call in 2006, I was soon persuaded that it was genuine and duly attended a presentation in Birmingham to receive the cheque for £1,000 and a citation for 'Taking a Stand'. Ben Sullivan also received a similar award in 2007, and between us we bought litter sticks, contributed to a local 'Neighbourhood Police' computer and helped several good causes, including an active youth worker. We appreciated all the recognition for Pensioners Against Litter, and we will continue the work for as long as we are able.

Printed in the United Kingdom
by Lightning Source UK Ltd.
134028UK00001B/234/P